BLACK&DECKER®

THE COMPLETE GUIDE TO

A CLUTTER-FREE
HOME

Organized Storage Solutions & Projects

by Philip Schmidt

**Creative Publishing
international**

MINNEAPOLIS, MINNESOTA
www.creativepub.com

Creative Publishing
international

Copyright © 2009
Creative Publishing international, Inc.
400 First Avenue North, Suite 300
Minneapolis, Minnesota 55401
1-800-328-0590
www.creativepub.com
All rights reserved

Printed in China

10 9 8 7 6 5 4 3 2

Library of Congress Cataloging-in-Publication Data

Schmidt, Philip.
  The complete guide to a clutter-free home : organized storage
solutions & projects / by Philip Schmidt.
      p. cm.
  At head of title: Branded by Black & Decker
  Includes index.
  Summary: "Includes strategies, ideas and step-by-step how to projects
that offer creative storage solutions to help control household
clutter"--Provided by publisher.
  ISBN-13: 978-1-58923-478-9 (soft cover)
  ISBN-10: 1-58923-478-2 (soft cover)
  1. Storage in the home. 2. House cleaning. 3. Orderliness. I.
Title. II. Title: Organized storage solutions & projects. III. Title:
Organized storage solutions and projects. IV. Title: Branded by Black &
Decker.
  TX309.S32 2009
  648'.8--dc22
                    2009028981

President/CEO: Ken Fund
VP for Sales & Marketing: Kevin Hamric

Home Improvement Group

Publisher: Bryan Trandem
Managing Editor: Tracy Stanley
Senior Editor: Mark Johanson
Editor: Jennifer Gehlhar

Creative Director: Michele Lanci-Altomare
Senior Design Managers: Jon Simpson, Brad Springer
Design Managers: James Kegley

Lead Photographer: Joel Schnell
Shop Assistant: Cesar Fernandez Rodriguez

Production Managers: Linda Halls, Laura Hokkanen

Page Layout Artist: Tiffany Laschinger
Shop Help: Charlie Boldt

The Complete Guide to a Clutter-Free Home
Created by: The Editors of Creative Publishing international, Inc., in cooperation with Black & Decker.
Black & Decker® is a trademark of The Black & Decker Corporation and is used under license.

NOTICE TO READERS

For safety, use caution, care, and good judgment when following the procedures described in this book. The publisher and Black & Decker cannot assume responsibility for any damage to property or injury to persons as a result of misuse of the information provided.

The techniques shown in this book are general techniques for various applications. In some instances, additional techniques not shown in this book may be required. Always follow manufacturers' instructions included with products, since deviating from the directions may void warranties. The projects in this book vary widely as to skill levels required: some may not be appropriate for all do-it-yourselfers, and some may require professional help.

Consult your local building department for information on building permits, codes, and other laws as they apply to your project.

Contents

The Complete Guide to a Clutter-free Home

Introduction

What makes this book different from the many other books about home organization and storage? Simple: it not only guides you through the process of decluttering and organizing your home from top to bottom, it also shows you how to create dozens of innovative storage solutions for maintaining order in every room in the house. It isn't simply a bunch of commonsense tips you've heard a thousand times, illustrated with some old photos that resemble your parent's or grandparent's house. Nor is it an entry-level woodworking book with black and white diagrams showing you how to build six different spice racks. *The Complete Guide to a Clutter-free Home* is a practical guide intended for the enthusiastic do-it-yourselfer whose goal is to create an efficient, visually pleasing home for today, where every item has its place.

Since you're thinking about home organization, and perhaps have even slipped into daydreams about a blissful, clutter-free existence, you've surely wondered what the secret is to keeping everything in its place: Better storage containers? More closet space? A remodeled kitchen? A bigger house? Of course, having more space and more places to put things might help, but only temporarily. The fact is, a three-story home can have as many storage challenges as a one-bedroom apartment, it's just that one can be crammed with a lot more clutter than the other. The real secret to a well-organized home lies in a process of analyzing your everyday activities and finding storage solutions that make it all work better.

To be sure, part of that process is weeding through all the junk you've been diverting to piles in recent months or years. This follows a process of its own, which you'll learn about in the first chapter. But soon enough you'll come to the more thoughtful work of devising a storage plan for each room, and then creating or choosing the best projects or products to meet your needs.

As you work toward your goal of a clutter-free home, it will help to remember that organization is always a work in progress. Don't expect a global transformation to happen overnight or even over a long weekend. Once you get started, you'll find that much of the organizing work involves adopting a new way of thinking in addition to seeking the right place for everything. You'll also find that each accomplishment, no matter how small, will motivate you to do more. Try to set a doable goal for each block of time you have available, and focus on tackling a specific area before moving to the next. Like any big project, household clutter is best managed one step at a time.

The photos on the next few pages will help inspire you to get the ball rolling and take control of the clutter in your home.

Gallery of Storage Success

This versatile kitchen island is a one-man-band of clever space utilization. It includes a prep surface for the cook, a breakfast bar for the family, and a spacious storage alcove that is put to good use as an entertainment center. It also creates a visual barrier that helps segregate any kitchen mess from the other living spaces.

This easy add-on to the end of an upper cabinet run takes pressure off the horizontal surfaces below, where the various notepads, keys, and pencil holders would otherwise reside.

Slide-out cabinet storage units are exploding in popularity, both in the initial design of custom cabinets and as retrofits to existing cabinetry. Finally, hard-to-store smallware like baking sheets and cutting boards have a convenient place for safe keeping.

Installing closet organizing systems is a fast-growing industry with technicians who can make a huge improvement in the usability of everything from a small reach-in closet to an adjoining bedroom that's reconfigured as a walk-in closet. Most building centers carry all the materials you need to create a closet system yourself.

Keep it small. Fitting a closet with a lot of small cubbies and drawers may not be the most efficient way to use your space, but it prevents your closet from turning into a loose collection of junk drawers with no good organizational system.

There are many accessories available for closet storage systems, but the most common are pullout belt (as shown) and scarf (inset) racks. There are also extendable pant racks that glide out, sunglass storage, hat storage, and more. And never underestimate the value of adding a few simple hooks to any outside shelving or cabinet side.

A bed surround occupying an entire wall has a dramatic design impact on a room while offering up plenty of storage for a minimal sacrifice of floor space. You can use stock cabinets to build your own surround, or have a custom unit built for you. Consider incorporating a reading light or two into the design.

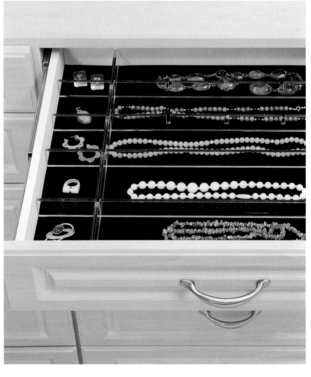

Jewelry drawers with dividers are useful cabinet features. They keep your valuables organized and out of sight, plus they eliminate the need to clutter up your dresser top with a jewelry chest. Soft drawer bottom liners are also available.

A traditional media center combines media storage with display storage and is designed to blend in with the trim and millwork in the room. Adding a soffit above the media center turns it into a bona fide built-in, and the soffit space can be used to run cables or to house recessed speakers.

Even flat screen TVs present a major storage issue because of the attendant clutter they attract. This entertainment center contains some storage spaces for items you want left out in plain view, such as electronic media players, while offering hidden storage spaces so elements such as DVDs can be kept behind doors.

A well-planned home office or craft center has a dedicated spot for just about everything. A slat wall with hangers, baskets, and shelves is easy to customize to your needs. Adjustable shelving also lets you rearrange your storage configurations as needed.

Here, cubbies were made for storing printed matter, be it mail, magazines, newspapers, or important printed forms. Obviously, they can hold nonprinted matter as well. Building cubbies from scratch is a bit tricky, but you can find ready-to-assemble cubby systems that are very easy to work with.

Maximize storage space in attics and under stairs so the overhead angles do not create obstacles. The attic system here makes use of practically every inch of space in a cramped corner.

The garage has great storage potential, but unless you're careful you can easily end up with a bunch of boxes and nowhere to park your car. Most building centers now carry a full line of products to help you organize your garage into an efficient storage area.

The entry area to your house should be equipped with plenty of accessible and attractive storage space. Ideally, each family member will have a dedicated area within the larger storage component. Because first impressions count, make sure your entry storage is attractive as well as functional.

Clutter management is partly about storing things and partly about protecting usable space so it stays usable. This garage is a perfect example. Here, the storage cabinets and wall hanging systems leave the floor free and open up countertop space.

Address the Mess

Tackling clutter is the first step to achieving an organized home. In this chapter we'll cover the all-important work of paring down your stuff to keep only the things you really need, really use, and really love. As for the rest, you can send it out the door to the landfill, to a friend or charity, or, if you absolutely can't part with it, into long-term storage. Because a cluttered home can never be an organized home, you have to pitch before you can progress.

The next step is to examine how you use each room in your home. Are your things where they need to be, close to where you use them most often? Are there conflicts within spaces that lead to clutter and inefficiency, such as a family room that serves as living space, home office, and kids' play headquarters? Where does clutter tend to grow the fastest and why?

Finally, we'll discuss some techniques for maintaining order in your newly organized spaces. With the right storage systems in place, you'll find that keeping ahead of clutter is all about good habits, not about changing who you are. In other words, you don't have to be a born neatnik to make it work (although you will have to get all the other slobs in the house to follow the plan).

In this chapter:
- The Problem with Clutter
- Decluttering Your Home
- Maintaining Order

The Problem with Clutter

Before we get into a full-scale character attack on clutter and what it does to our homes and happiness, let's start by defining what clutter really is. Clutter is not just stuff that's disorganized or out of place, like the rolls of holiday wrapping paper stashed behind your office door or last year's tax returns covering every inch of the dining room table. Clutter is also the direct result of a slow but steady accumulation of things that we didn't ask for, shouldn't have bought, or no longer need.

Clutter is gifts that we keep out of guilt, like that horribly tacky party tray from your sister-in-law (which you strongly suspect was regifted). Clutter is broken things that you never got around to fixing. Clutter is bits and pieces of nostalgia that you hoard for posterity. In short, clutter is all the stuff that you'd get rid of or move to a more suitable place if you only had the time to go through it and the will to make the tough decision to toss.

So, aside from how it looks, why is clutter so bad? For starters, it affects us all in both practical and psychological ways. It doesn't just fill our living spaces; it fills our minds. Seeing a jumble of misplaced items in every room is a constant reminder of unfinished business and unresolved issues. All this emotional baggage weighs heavily on the spirit, sapping our energy and possibly keeping us from doing something new, something positive.

The practical effects of clutter are more obvious. You simply can't live and work efficiently or peacefully in your home when the traffic routes are blocked with laundry and every flat surface is covered with old papers. Clutter makes everyday things (car keys) hard to find and time-sensitive things (mortgage bills) easy to forget. Perhaps most important, clutter takes up valuable storage and display space where cherished and truly useful items could go. That's why you have to minimize your clutter before you can plan new storage systems. If you don't, you'll just be bailing out a sinking boat by moving the water from bow to stern.

One person's clutter is another person's treasure. The first step in any serious effort to make your home clutter-free is to sit down with everyone in the household, negotiate, and settle on a definition of clutter that works for everyone.

Clutter is the slow accumulation of unwanted paperwork or items that are an inevitable byproduct of our lives. The act of managing this byproduct is the first step to decluttering.

Clutter eventually becomes its own problem. Before a cleanup, this guest room served only as a huge receptacle for miscellaneous stuff. Taking the time to pitch unwanted junk and organizing the space with efficient storage and a work area transformed it into a pleasant guest room that also serves as a home office.

Decluttering Your Home

As evidenced by the numerous books and television shows about home organization, decluttering is much more than tidying up around the house. It's also distinctly different from spring cleaning. Cleaning is, for the most part, mindless manual labor (which is probably why many people find it so therapeutic). Decluttering is all about making decisions: Will I ever read this book again or should I donate it to the library? Where can I store these craft supplies so my visiting relatives don't have to trip over them? Am I really attached to all of my grandfather's old hats, or will one or two preserve his memory just as well? Why is this house such a wreck all of the time?

Decluttering is finally saying "the buck stops here," with the primary goal of regaining control of your household and, consequently, a big part of your home life. The work is at times difficult and exhausting, but the rewards are almost guaranteed to exceed your expectations. No one knows this better than professional organizers: people who earn a living by helping others make decisions about their own stuff.

Organizing experts work from different philosophies and methods. Some adhere to the principles of feng shui and help clients improve the flow of positive energy in their homes through decluttering, furniture arrangement, and other techniques. Other pros focus more on practical goals than spiritual ones. All, however, recommend a systematic approach to decluttering. They know from experience how hard it is to succeed without some guidelines and planning. Following are some tried-and-true tips from the gurus of home organization.

Make it Fun for the Whole Family ▶

Most experts recommend having kids declutter their own rooms, play areas, and toy collections. This promotes a sense of responsibility for managing their stuff, and it gives them a say in what stays and what goes. It's also the best way to get them involved in ongoing clutter maintenance.

If it's not trash, it either stays in the room or goes into one of three boxes. Sticking to this rule helps you make a decision on the spot.

You can motivate children to part with toys by holding a contest—the one who purges the most stuff wins a prize. Reward everyone involved (including yourself) in the big clear-out.

The Decluttering Process

The goal of decluttering is to get rid of excess stuff until you're left with only the things you really need, use, and love. You will also move items to the places where they really belong. This prepares you for the next big step of organizing and storing your things in each space so everything looks and works just right. Start by breaking up the job into smaller tasks. For the initial battle of sorting and pitching, arm yourself with these tools:

1. Boxes or trash bags for throw-away junk
2. A "donate" box for items you'll take to a local charity
3. A "return" box for items that belong to someone else and for things that you want to give away to friends
4. A "relocate" box for items that you're keeping but that belong in another room or area of the house
5. Optional: A "sell" box for any valuable items you'd like to resell for cash

At the end of each decluttering session, do the following:

- Take out the trash. Don't leave your boxes and bags sitting in the house.

- Put your donate and return boxes in your car, preferably in the passenger's seat. This forces you to deal with them soon and prevents you from driving by your friend's house or the charity thrift shop without your drop-off items.
- Walk through the house with the relocate box and deliver everything to its proper location.

Set a goal for each sorting session, whether its organizing one shelf in the library or tackling the hall closet, and finish the job completely before starting somewhere else. When each area is decluttered—and, ideally, cleaned—put away the broom and other cleaning supplies that you used. Leaving them out and in the way will only create more clutter and detract from your sense of satisfaction in a job well done.

For big jobs, schedule plenty of time to complete the task at hand. Treat the session as a work day by starting early and taking as few breaks as possible. Scheduling is especially important if roommates or other family members are involved in the effort. Kids who are old enough definitely should take part in helping out. However, for some stages of the process, it might be wise to arrange for your kids to sleep over at a friend's house.

Start small. Before tackling surface clutter it's a good idea to clear out dedicated storage areas, like file cabinets and junk drawers. This makes room for stowing the current stuff that you're more likely to keep for a while.

Getting Started ▶

You don't need a grand, comprehensive plan to start decluttering. You can begin with any part of the house, but preferably those areas that bother you the most. Try to save the worst clutter spots—the garage, basement, storage shed, etc.—for later in the process. If you're especially pressed for time, tackle something small, like a single kitchen cabinet or a bathroom drawer. You'll be amazed at how much this motivates you to do more.

Next, set your sights on an entire room or just part of a room. Your own bedroom is a good place to start, as you'll quickly create a sanctuary that gives you a jolt of decluttering energy each time you're in it. Whenever possible, clear clutter at the time of day when you're best equipped to make decisions. If you're a morning person and do your best work in the early hours, don't wait until nighttime to start rummaging. Decisiveness is the key to working effectively.

One of the best methods for helping to decide what to do with an item is to ask yourself how the thing makes you feel when you see it. If it brings up memories of a fun trip or a happy time in your life and it's attractive, it might be a good candidate for a display item. If, on the other hand, it's a gift from someone you don't particularly like but you feel obliged to keep it, perhaps you can relieve yourself of the guilt (and the item) by giving it away to someone who will really enjoy it. Our homes are full of things that conjure up feelings of one kind or another (often unexpectedly as we glimpse them in passing). Considering each item for its positive impact on your everyday life is a good way to decide what stays out, what goes into storage, and what you'd be better off cleansing from your house and mind forever.

Most home organization professionals urge their clients to set time limits for usable items, reasoning that if they haven't used something in six months or a year they probably never will and should get rid of it. A time limit is an effective measure for a lot of household clutter, such as single-purpose kitchen tools that you bought on a whim (or received as a gift) but have never used. Setting a one-year limit on everyday clothing is also a good idea. Other items aren't so well suited to the time limit test. For example, if you bought a plumbing snake to clear a drain a while back and you've been lucky enough not to have needed it since, you'd still want to keep it because clogged drains are a fact of life and you'll need that snake sooner or later.

Another test for assessing clutter involves replacement cost versus real-life value. If you think of storage space in your home as having value, how much is it costing you to keep inexpensive items that you'll probably never need again? This is a good test for people who tend to hang onto leftover building and landscape materials. For example, a new sheet of drywall costs about six dollars. A partial sheet leftover from your basement remodel is worth even less. Throwing out the drywall cutoffs is a good investment, since the value of the storage space they occupy is worth far more than the replacement cost of new material.

Touch It Once—Don't Procrastinate! ▶

Efficient business people and office workers apply this rule to paperwork every day. When you pick something up, make a decision about it—put it away or into the appropriate box—and move on. Deferring the decision for later quickly becomes a bad habit that will leave you with a huge pile of work at the end of the day.

Try this time limit test for clothing: Face all of your hanging clothes in one direction. Each time you wear an item, hang it back up in the opposite direction. At the end of a year, all items still facing the original direction probably belong in the donate box.

Compartment systems in junk drawers and other miscellaneous storage spaces prevent your catch-all junk drawers from becoming clutter bins.

You will start noticing a lot more of these collection bins around town once decluttering is on your mind. Be sure your items for donation are clean and in good repair before dropping them off.

Keep Your Eye on the Ball ▸

Decluttering is not the time to read old love letters or look up friends in your high school yearbook, as this is a sure way to bring the cleanup day to a screeching halt. Save the trip down memory lane for after your house is in order. If you feel you must review some old things before deciding their fate, put them in a box (a small one, preferably) and commit to going through it more thoroughly immediately after you've organized everything else.

It's okay if you want to cling to some catch-all places, like a junk drawer or a toy chest. These are necessary parts of most home storage plans. Of course, these areas tend to accumulate clutter faster than anywhere else, so it's a good idea to go through them and pitch stuff frequently. Likewise, it's okay to have everyday items that you frequently use out in the open as long as they're in a convenient location. Your house may never be a candidate for a cover story in *Metropolitan Home*, and it can look as "lived in" as you like. Just make sure the stuff that's out isn't getting in the way of your normal activities.

Charity organizations make it incredibly easy to donate all sorts of household goods. Many will even send a truck to your house to pick up big stuff, like couches and other furniture. Otherwise, you can drop off clothing, books, toys, games, small appliances, and dishware at thrift outlets, churches, homeless shelters, and other charitable organizations. Just look through

the phone book or do an Internet search to find out which places are set up to accept donations. If you have some nice suits and other business attire to give away, find a local back-to-work program that helps outfit clients for job interviews.

Donating goods not only aids those in need, it also helps to reduce clutter in the big picture and keeps more stuff out of the landfill. Since many charitable donations are tax-deductible, ask your tax preparer about keeping records of your donations. In general, you should record a description and estimated market value for each item, the date of donation, and the name and tax identification number of the charity.

Choosing to donate can also help you make tough decluttering decisions. If guilt has prevented you from throwing out gifts you don't use or clothes your kids have outgrown, you can feel good about giving the items to someone who really needs them, making your decision to purge that much easier.

Turning Clutter Into Cash ▸

Can't decide what to do with that nice, hand-me-down coffee table from your folks that never quite fit in your living room? What about the elaborate beer-making kit that failed to turn you into the next great brewmaster? Today, the answer is simpler than ever: sell it online, through bartering and private auction websites. All you have to do is post a description (and perhaps a photo) of your item, and let the buyers come to you. Another option is to sell your stuff for cash at resellers like pawn shops, vintage clothing stores, second-hand stores, and antiques dealers, depending on the type of goods. Or you can put your things up for sale through a consignment shop, which might bring a better price than an immediate cash exchange. However, if you have loads of miscellaneous stuff to sell, you're probably better off pawning it the old-fashioned way, by holding a yard sale. Here are some tips for making the most of a sale:

- Before you plan the sale, make sure you have enough stuff—that is, enough potential income—to make the time and effort worthwhile. If your own collection of merchandise seems paltry, ask neighbors whether they'd like to join you or if they have any juicy items to add to your sale.

- Plan the sale for a Saturday (or Saturday and Sunday) that's not on a holiday weekend. Good weather is a must, and you'll just have to cross your fingers for that.

- Advertise like a pro. Create large, colorful signs with clear lettering (all signs should look the same), including directions, your address, and the sale date and hours. Post the signs on all major streets in the area.

- Organize and price-label all of your merchandise in your garage the night before the sale so you can start setting up at the crack of dawn. Yard sale junkies hit the streets early. You want your sale to appear chock-full of goodies so as not to lose drive-by customers.

- Assemble a staff of a few friends or family members to help meet the crowd and make quick sales.

- Prepare to bargain. You'll sell more stuff and have more fun doing it if you're willing to haggle a little over prices.

- Slash prices near the end of the day. Remember, the goal is to get rid of all your stuff. When it's all over, take unsold items to a charity drop-off, or set large pieces along the road with a Free! sign. You'll be amazed at how quickly the stuff will disappear.

If you post it, they will come. Advertising is the key to a successful yard sale.

Assessing Function

With the dreaded task of clutter clearing behind you, there's not only less stuff to deal with, in the process you've also inventoried everything you're keeping. But before you head to the store in search of bins and file boxes, take some time to brainstorm on the function of each room. The goal here is to make sure your stuff—and the work you do with it—is in the right place to begin with. For each main space, ask yourself these questions:

- How is the space currently used?
- What is the ideal use of the space?
- What changes do I need to make to meet the ideal (or at least get close to it)?

For example, let's say your formal dining room has become the default location for bill-paying and general household paperwork. If this function has prevented you from using the room for special meals, the current setup is less than ideal. What you need is a dedicated office space.

A little creative brainstorming and thoughtful planning will lead you to the right solution. Perhaps you can carve some space out of a corner of the kitchen or living room. Or maybe you can equip an extra bedroom to serve as both office and guest quarters. Is there an underused closet that can be converted to an office (see page 146)? If the dining room offers the only available space in the house, let it serve double duty by moving the paperwork and office tasks to a modified armoire or corner unit with doors. Simply shut the doors to restore the formal ambience for dining.

Taking a step back and thinking about organization and function in the bigger picture is the key to making the most of your home's available spaces. Once you've mapped out a plan for each room, you can narrow your focus to dealing with the stuff itself. The tips and projects in the following chapters will help you do just that.

Visualize Your Plans

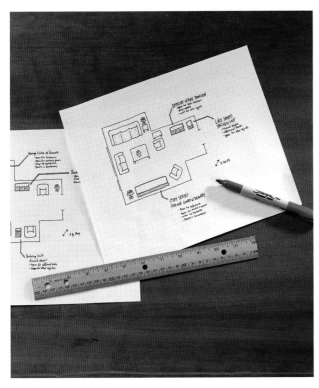

Try drawing a scaled floor plan of the space onto graph paper if you're having trouble visualizing major changes to a room's setup (left) . Add all furniture and other features that will stay, plus any new items for the proposed plan. Experiment with different layouts to find an arrangement that works. Alternatively, you can print out a photo of the room, then sketch ideas onto an overlay of vellum or tracing paper (right).

Maintaining Order

No matter how much stuff you purged in step one or how well you planned your new storage systems, you'll soon be right back where you started without a little discipline. That's the bad news. The good news is you don't have to be an organized person by nature to keep a tidy home. What you need are effective systems and handy storage spaces that allow you to take charge of your stuff with less effort.

Consider this real-life example: You're a passionate foodie who subscribes to several cooking magazines. You seldom have the time to read each issue before the next one arrives in the mail, so the old ones start to pile up. You might even leave new issues lying around in conspicuous places (like the kitchen table) to remind yourself to read them. Does this work? If it did, you wouldn't have a clutter problem.

Instead, store any unfinished magazines near your favorite reading chair. Don't worry, you won't forget they're there. And when you get a few moments to read, you won't waste precious time looking for them. The next problem to tackle is the inevitable stockpile of old, unread magazines at your reading spot. It's time to separate the wheat from the chaff: look through the table of contents in each issue and tear out the must-read articles and recipes. Recycle the rest of the magazine (at this point, it's mostly ads anyway). Prioritize the articles so you read those you're most interested in first, and file any recipes you really want to try. Now you've reduced a stack of old magazines to a handful of select pages.

The best storage solutions fit with your everyday life. If your kids' favorite place to play is the family room, that's probably where the toy bin should go.

Basic Principles of Organization ▸

1. **Efficiency follows reality.** Storage solutions must conform to the way you really live. If you tend to leave coats draped over kitchen chairs instead of hanging them in the coat closet, you need a better storage solution—perhaps some coat hooks or a coat tree next to the entry door.

2. **Store the most-used stuff close at hand.** Everyday cooking utensils and pots and pans should be reachable from the stove. Magazines and newspapers belong near your reading chair.

3. **Beware of container clutter.** Too many boxes, bins, and bags can lead to more clutter than the stuff itself. Weeding out excess items periodically and moving seldom-used things to long-term storage reduces the need for more storage vessels.

4. **Keep it simple.** Complicated storage systems are bound to be ignored, especially by kids.

5. **Leave room to grow.** Plan some extra room for the ebb and flow of accumulated stuff. Space flexibility helps contain clutter between periodic weed-out sessions.

6. **Never trust your memory.** Clearly label all boxes used for long-term storage, or use clear plastic bins that reveal the contents at a glance.

THE ONE-IN, ONE-OUT RULE.

Whenever you buy or acquire something new, particularly a nonnecessity, select one existing thing in your house to get rid of.

10-MINUTE DECLUTTER.

Devote 10 minutes each day to tackling your home's most common clutter, whether it's sorting the mail, gathering laundry, hanging clothes in your bedroom, recycling newspapers and magazines, or organizing your desk. Enforcing a 10-minute toy pickup is a good way to keep kids on track, too.

ANNUAL DECLUTTER.

Most people find the motivation for some kind of spring cleaning session. So now that you've learned the process (and benefits) of a whole-house decluttering, why not start your annual spring cleaning with a day of purging? The cleaning will go faster with less stuff in the way, and you'll break the pattern of steady unchecked accumulation each year.

JUST SAY NO (OR A FIRM MAYBE).

If you're prone to accepting hand-me-down items from friends and family on an impulse, try using this test: don't take the item home with you when it's first offered. Ask for a day or two before making a decision. Take measurements of the item (especially if it's furniture or anything large), then go home and make sure it fits the space you have planned for it. You'll be surprised at how often you say "no, thanks" after you've slept on the decision for a night.

Try to make regular organizing a fun challenge. Professional organizers often suggest setting a timer to help you move as quickly as possible on your daily decluttering blitz.

Kitchens

As the true hub of the modern home, the kitchen presents some unique challenges for the war on clutter. The biggest challenge is providing storage for a vast and complex assortment of food-related items, from frying pans and corkscrews to linens and dishware.

How and where all that stuff is stored is often the biggest factor in how smoothly a kitchen operates. In most kitchens, the storage systems consist of a set of cabinets and a pantry of some sort (if you're lucky). Cabinets hold a lot, but being little more than rectangular boxes, they're not as user-friendly or as space-efficient as they could be.

Making the most of this space requires some thoughtful rearranging to ensure everything is right where it belongs. Ordinary cabinets can use some help from simple add-ons and devices that improve access and visibility of stored items, in addition to bumping up their capacity. Where your existing storage spaces are falling short, a custom-built unit might do the trick, such as the pot rack on page 34 or the pantry project on page 44. If your kitchen is like most, it's ripe with opportunity for cutting clutter and improving organization.

In this chapter:

- Storage Strategies
- Pot Racks
- Slide-out Storage
- Pull-out Pantry
- Vertical Cabinet Dividers
- Dish Rack
- Pantry Shelf
- Pine Pantry
- Pull-down Shelves

Storage Strategies

With all that it's required to hold and do, a kitchen is a complicated room, to say the least. Space is at an absolute premium, and fitting in all the necessary tools and supplies in an organized manner can be like packing the trunk of a car for a long road trip.

To help you solve this spatial jigsaw puzzle, manufacturers and home centers offer an endless array of products designed for maximizing storage and minimizing clutter. These can do for an overloaded cabinet what a filing system does for a stack of paperwork. And where store-bought products don't quite fit your space or offer the look you're after, creating something of your own design (with a little help, of course) is always a good option.

As you dive into the details of organizing your kitchen, it's important to keep in mind the true purpose of this busiest of rooms. The kitchen is a work area, first and foremost. The more you can arrange and maintain the space for storing, cooking, and serving food, the better it will serve your household. Using the counters as a catchall for mail and newspapers, or the cabinets for storing light bulbs and holiday dishware, only means those spaces aren't available for work on a daily basis. Respect the kitchen as a workplace, and you'll find it much easier to control clutter and keep the stage set for fixing the next meal.

Open counter space is worth its weight in gold in any kitchen. Preventing clutter here is key to an efficient work space—and peace of mind.

Commercial kits make it easy to convert a narrow cabinet into an easy-access shelving unit. The shelf unit mounts to the cabinet box and has brackets for installing your own hardware.

Cooking Tools & Equipment

Follow two basic themes when organizing cooking equipment: point of use and frequency of use. When you need a whisk in a hurry because your cream sauce is starting to separate, is the tool right at your fingertips or is it buried deep in a drawer on the far side of the sink? The point of use rule dictates that the most-used tools belong next to the stove or cooktop.

Frequency of use is just as straightforward: everyday pots and pans belong right in the cooking area, preferably hung on a pot rack. Give less priority to occasional-use pieces, such as double boilers, stockpots, and roasting pans (depending on the type of cooking you do). In general, each item should have to earn its place. If you haven't used an item in a year or more, consider getting rid of it or storing it in a less-convenient location. Pieces that come out only for specific holiday meals might be best stowed in long-term storage with the rest of the holiday stuff.

Pull-out trays or shallow drawers are great for organizing equipment and small appliances in large base cabinets. The pull-out feature makes for easy access and eliminates digging for pieces in the back of the cabinet. Cookie sheets, cutting boards, and other flat items are best stored on-edge. You can outfit cabinets with commercial racks or install custom-fit, full-height dividers (see page 47). If you have open space above your wall cabinets, you can use it for storing (and displaying) infrequently used cookware, serving pieces, or dishware propped against the wall and held with a piece of trim.

Dishware

Finding room for every piece of dishware can really put your spatial and organizational skills to the test. Everyday pottery should go where it's easy to reach for both serving meals and unloading the dishwasher. Although most people do it, it's difficult to store all of your dishware in close proximity. It's better to separate the everyday stuff from the occasional-use pieces and store the latter in less convenient locations. Here are some other tips that can help:

- Wire stands (sometimes called shelf expanders) help separate small stacks of dishware, so you don't have to pull down a tall, heavy stack to get to pieces at the bottom.
- Teacups and coffee mugs can hang from cup hooks screwed into the bottoms of shelves. The space below can hold more mugs or stacks of plates and saucers.
- Fine dinnerware, glassware, and china are better stored away from the everyday stuff, where it's out of the way and safe from breakage. Container stores sell padded cases for safely storing fine pieces. Same goes for good silverware and serving pieces.
- Deep drawers with heavy-duty glides can be fitted with plate organizers. These eliminate the heavy lifting required when dishware is stored in wall cabinets.
- Good kitchen knives belong in a knife block or on a wall-mounted holder nearest the food prep area. In-drawer holders are good, too, if they're easy to access and you can spare the space.

A sturdy metal canister or ceramic pitcher next to the cooktop is ideal for storing spatulas, spoons, and whisks at the ready. Another option is to hang the tools from a wall-mounted bar or rack.

Cookbooks don't get top billing in most kitchens, but some cooks like to keep their favorites close at hand. Here, a lesser-used cabinet had its doors removed to create a bookshelf.

Simple accessories like dish racks, shelf expanders, cup hooks, and placemat racks make the most of primary cabinet space and keep everyday dishware in one convenient location.

Dry Food & Spices

For most cooks, organizing foodstuffs, cooking oils, and spices is as much an issue of visibility as it is of space. How often do you make emergency runs to the grocery store because you've suddenly run out of flour? Or how much time do you spend searching for that one critical spice? The solution is to arrange supplies efficiently while keeping every item in view.

Dry foods and baking supplies work best on shallow shelves lining the walls of a pantry or in pull-out trays or drawers in cabinetry (see pages 40 to 43). If you don't have a bona fide pantry, perhaps you can install pantry-style shelves in a nearby closet. For spices, visibility and easy access are key. Shallow spice racks can mount inside cabinet doors or onto the backsplash wall space between the countertop and wall cabinets. For drawer storage, transfer spices to identical shaker jars and write the name of each spice onto the jar cap.

Keep baking staples like flour, meal, and sugar in clear containers so you can see when supplies are getting low. This also eliminates the mess of paper bags. Just make sure the containers have large openings so you can easily reach in with a measuring cup.

These days, lots of people buy in bulk, which saves money but creates a super-sized storage problem. One solution is to designate an out-of-the-way storage area—in a laundry room, utility room, or the garage—and use it like a merchant's stock room: With all of the bulk items stored in one place, you always know where to go for backup supplies. Basement stairway shelves are another good option for bulk-food storage.

To keep spices out of the way but clearly in view, store them in clear-top, magnetic spice tins stuck to a custom-cut metal sheet or store-bought strips mounted to the backsplash area near your cooking surface.

Classic pantry shelving can be built with 1 × 6 boards mounted to 1 × 1 or 1 × 2 wall cleats. Include short shelves for canned goods and taller shelves for flour bins and cereal boxes. High shelves are good for storing occasional-use items.

For concealed storage consider using DIY kits on the inside of cabinet faces. They are available in many styles and finishes. Consult the manufacturer's instructions for installation and weight capacities.

Cleanup & Recycling

With recycling now standard practice in the kitchen, the single trash bin stashed under the sink just isn't enough (it never was terribly convenient anyway). Today's solution to disposal is to group the trash and recycling in one easy-access location. The best option is to install a pull-out rack system in a base cabinet for holding all necessary bins (you have to give up some cabinet space, but it's worth it).

As for that freed-up space under the sink, a pull-out wire basket is perfect for organizing cleaning supplies and dish detergent, and you never again have to grope around for items in the back of this cumbersome and often cruddy cabinet space. To help keep your sink-top area clean and uncluttered, install a tilt-out tray behind the false drawer front on the sink-base cabinet. This simple system mounts to the cabinet frame and drawer front. Concealed-hinge trays are completely hidden when closed.

Utility closets, broom closets, laundry room storage areas and the like can all benefit from closet systems and components. Let point of use and frequency of use guide your organization plan in these everyday work areas.

Three simple ways to improve kitchen cleanup: pull-out trash and recycling bins (bottom); pull-out under-sink organizer (middle); false front tilt-out tray (top).

Pot Racks

Pot racks free up loads of cabinet space and save you time during cooking. The storage shelf above can hold anything else you like to have at the ready.

Nothing eats up valuable cabinet space like a full set of pots and pans. And for cooks who like to get serious in the kitchen, rummaging through stacks of pans in the heat of preparation is a major inconvenience. That's why many home chefs prefer to store their most-used cookware on an overhead rack, where all of the pieces are visible at a glance and you can easily reach up and pluck down what you need without having to search through a cabinet.

The three custom pot racks shown on the following pages combine the space-saving convenience of pot hangers with a deep storage shelf above—perfect for storing stock pots and other hard-to-hang pieces or a collection of your favorite cookbooks. The simple designs can be customized with any finish and hardware you like, and you can size your unit to fit any

space in your kitchen. Because the racks are wallhung, you don't need an island or a high ceiling, like you do with many ceiling-hung pot systems.

All of the materials for these racks are available at most home centers and hardware stores. You can also shop online to choose from a wide range of specialty hardware, including shelf brackets, hanging rods, and hooks in various materials and finishes such as stainless steel, wrought iron, nickel, chrome, and brass. For a built-in look, choose a shelf material and finish that matches your kitchen's cabinets and woodwork. Lumberyards and hardwood suppliers carry solid and edge-glued 1 × 12 stock in almost any species of wood. For a painted shelf, use ¾" poplar, or use basic melamine-coated shelf stock and leave it unpainted.

Hanger-rod Pot Rack

This design features a standard-size closet rod supported by two shelf-and-rod brackets. Home centers carry the 1⅝"-diameter closet rod in chrome, painted steel, and wood, and you can find other finishes online. Chrome and brushed nickel rods look good with sleek decorative brackets, also available online. For the individual pot hangers, you can use standard S-hooks so the pots face out, or combine rings and S-hooks so the pots face to the side for greater storage capacity.

Tools & Materials ▸

Work Gloves
Eye Protection
Circular saw
Straightedge
Orbital sander
Hacksaw
Drill driver
Metal file
Closet rod
Brackets
S-hooks
Wood screws
Finishing tools

¾" Finish-grade oak
  shelving (or shelf
  stock as desired)
Finish materials
Decorative rod
  end caps
Construction adhesive

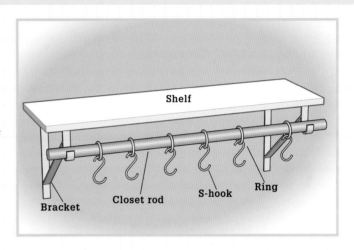

How to Build the Hanger-rod Pot Rack

1

Cut the shelf to the desired length using a circular saw and edge guide. Sand smooth and finish the shelf with three coats of polyurethane, or paint it with primer/sealer and two or more top coats. Cut the closet rod to length with a hacksaw. File the cut edges as needed.

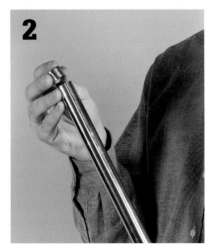

2

Cover the ends with decorative end caps. *Tip: Your pot rack will look best if the rod is a little bit shorter than the shelf.*

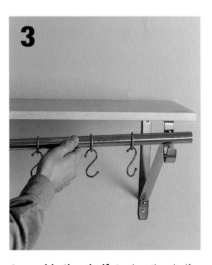

3

Assemble the shelf. Anchor the shelf brackets to the wall studs with screws, making sure the tops are perfectly level with each other. Attach the shelf to the brackets with screws. Add hooks to the rod, and then set the rod on the brackets with dabs of construction adhesive to prevent movement.

Suspended-shelf Pot Rack

A variation on standard shelf construction, the suspended shelf design has its shelf mounted to the bottoms of inverted brackets. Inverting the brackets gives you built-in bookends above the shelf and leaves the pot area below open for easy access. Large decorative key hooks or cup hooks serve as fixed hangers for the pots. Remember, this rack should only be used for lightweight cookware or cups.

Tools & Materials ▶

Circular saw
Straightedge
Level
Drill/driver
Pliers or socket wrenches
Panhead screws
Panhead bolts and nuts

¾" finish-grade oak shelving (or shelf stock as desired)
Cup hooks (5)
Shelf brackets (2)
Wall anchors

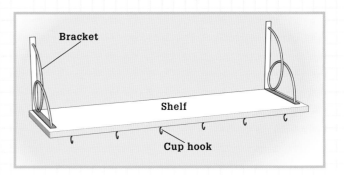

How to Build the Suspended-shelf Pot Rack

1

Cut the shelf to length and finish as desired (see Step 1 on page 35). Install the cup hooks with even spacing on the bottom face of the shelf. Make sure there's enough room so your largest pan won't touch the wall.

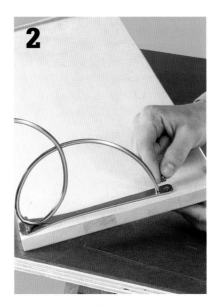

2

Secure the brackets to the shelf with nice-looking panhead (or other) machine bolts and nuts. The bolt heads should go on the bottom of the shelf, and the threaded ends should be flush with the top of the nuts.

3

Fasten the brackets to the wall with heavy-duty panhead (or other) wood screws. Make sure the shelf is perfectly level and drive the screws into wall studs or use heavy-duty, hollow wall anchors.

Built-in Pot Rack

The built-in rack is designed to span between two wall cabinets or between a cabinet and nearby wall. You can also use the same basic construction to build a large triangular corner shelf between two adjacent walls.

The pot rack shown here is made with metal tubing secured to the shelf with matching railing brackets. An alternative option is to install individual pot hooks as shown in the Suspended-shelf Pot Rack (page 36).

Tools & Materials ▶

Work Gloves
Eye Protection
Level
Drill
Circular saw
Miter saw
Pipe cutter
Nail set
Hammer
Finishing tools
¾" finished wood (shelving)
Molding (for cleats)
Finish screws and nails
Metal tubing and brackets
S-hooks or rings
Finishing materials

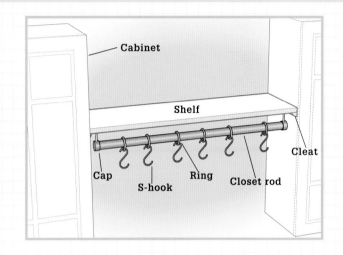

How to Build the Built-in Pot Rack

1

Install the cleats flush with the level lines using finish screws. Draw a level line along the wall and supporting cabinets ¾" below the desired height for the top of the shelf. Finish the molding for the cleats as desired and cut to length, mitering the inside corners and beveling the exposed front ends at 30°. Cut the shelf to fit snugly between the cabinets. Finish the shelf as desired.

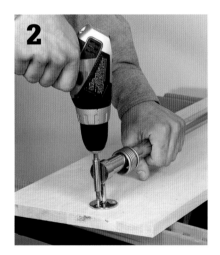

2

Cut the tubing to length with a plumber's pipe cutter. Add rings and/or S-hooks for the pot hooks (see page 36). Fit the railing brackets over the ends of the tubing and mount them to the shelf bottom with screws.

3

Set the shelf in place, and then fasten it to the cleats with finish nails driven through pilot holes.

Wooden Ladder Pot Rack

This inexpensive, easy-to-build pot rack is a wonderful organizer and great addition to any kitchen, especially kitchens that suffer from limited cabinet or countertop space. Most busy cooks have one or more overhead racks in their kitchens to keep frequently used cooking utensils within reach. Overhead racks also give proud cooks an opportunity to show off gourmet pans and other high-end cooking equipment.

The project shown here is a ladder-style rack made with wood dowels, from which the pots are hung with pot hooks. For an interesting variation, try building the rack with a ladder made with ¾" (or 1" if you can find it) metal electrical conduit. When sanded, the conduit has a matte finish similar to brushed aluminum or stainless steel.

A solid oak ladder with round rungs makes an intriguing kitchen pot rack that's easy to build.

Tools, Materials & Cutting List ▸

Tools

Work Gloves
Eye Protection
Circular saw and straightedge
Drill with 1" bit
Finish sander
Clamps
Portable drill guide
Nail set
Hammer
Wood mallet

Materials

16 ft. decorative chain
1 × 3" × 8 ft. oak (1)
1"-dia. × 3 ft. oak dowel (3)
J-hooks (to hang pots) (4)
Eye hooks (4)
Backer board
4d finish nails
Wood glue
Finishing materials

Key	Part	Dimension
A	(2) Stretcher	¾ × 2½" × 3 ft. oak
B	(5) Dowel	1"-dia. × 18" dowel

1½" (typ.)

A

B

8"

8"

8"

8"

B

B

How to Build the Wooden Ladder Pot Rack

Make the stretchers. Cut your hardwood stock to size (here, ¾ × 2½") and then cut the stretchers to length. Drill 1"-dia. holes in the stretchers spaced 8" apart on-center (See Diagram above). To ensure that the holes align, gang the stretchers together with their ends flush. Use a backer board to prevent drill tearout.

Ganged stretchers

Backer board

Assemble the ladder. Cut 1" doweling to length (we used oak stretchers and oak doweling, which is relatively easy to find). Sand all parts. Insert the dowels into the holes in the stretchers. Make sure the amount of dowel projecting out from each hole is uniform. Secure the dowels with glue and a single 4d finish nail driven through a pilot hole in the stretcher edge and into the dowel, pinning it. Hang from ceiling joists with chains.

Slide-out Storage

A base cabinet with slide-out trays or shelves is one of those great modern conveniences that has become standard in new kitchen design. Not only do slide-out trays make reaching stored items easier than with standard cabinet spaces—no more crouching and diving into the deep recesses of cavernous low shelves—they also store more items far more efficiently. With a few shallow trays, a standard base cabinet can hold dozens of food cans and still leave room for tall items like cereal boxes and bags of flour or even deep pots and countertop appliances.

To get the most from your new slide-out system, think carefully about how you will use each tray. Measure the items you're most likely to store together, and let the items dictate the spacing of the trays. Most standard base cabinets are suitable for trays. Wide cabinets (24" or wider) without a center partition (middle stile) are best in terms of space usage, but trays in narrow (18"-wide) cabinets are just as handy. If you have a wide cabinet with a middle stile, you can add trays along one or both sides of the stile. For economy and simplicity, the trays in this project are made with ¾"-thick plywood parts joined with glue and finish

nails. If you prefer a more finished look (not that there's anything wrong with the look of nice plywood), you can use 1 × 4 hardwood stock for the tray sides and set a ⅜"-thick plywood bottom panel into dadoes milled into the side pieces. Another option is to assemble plywood tray pieces using pocket screws so the screw heads don't show on the front pieces of the trays.

Tools & Materials ▸

Work Gloves	Drawer slides
Eye Protection	(1 set per tray)
Framing square	1 × 2 poplar (or other
Circular saw with	hardwood to match
straightedge guide	trays, if desired)
or table saw	¾" finish-grade plywood
Drill	Wood glue
Level	6d finish nails (or
Tape measure	pneumatic brads)
Hammer	Wood screws
Clamps	Finish materials

Slide-out trays eliminate the everyday problem of hard-to-reach and hard-to-see spaces in standard base cabinets. Better still, you can install your trays to accommodate the stuff you use most often.

Drawer Slides

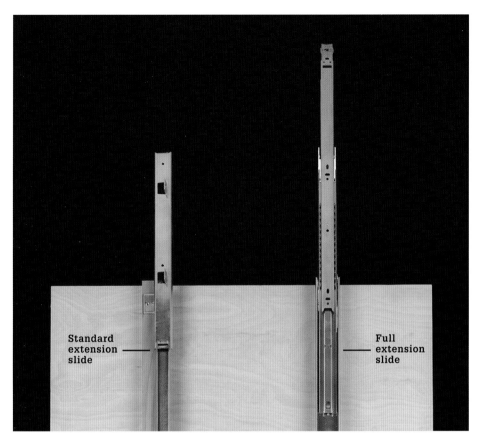

Drawer slides suitable for pullout shelves are commonly available in both standard (left) and full extension (right) styles. Standard slides are less expensive and good enough for most applications—they allow the tray to be pulled out most of the way. Full extension slides are a little pricier than standard slides, but they allow the tray to be pulled completely out of the cabinet box for easy access to items in the back.

Standard extension slide

Full extension slide

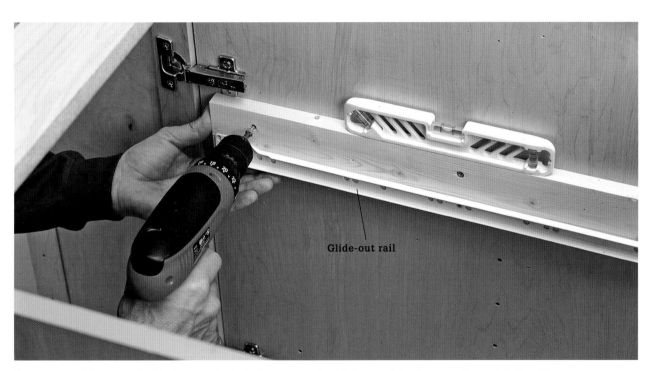

Glide-out rail

Spacers must be mounted to the cabinets before you can install drawer slides for your glide-out shelves. They are necessary for the drawers to clear the cabinet face frame and the door. For ¾" spacers, a 1 × 2, 1 × 3, or 1 × 4 works well. Paint or finish it to match the cabinet interior.

How to Install Slide-out Cabinet Trays

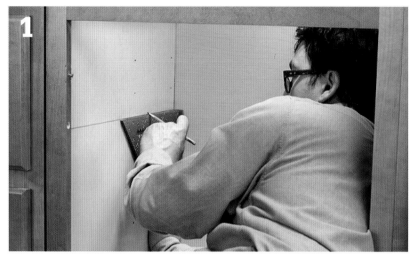

Lay out the tray positions, starting with the bottom tray. Check the drawer slides to see how much clearance you need for the bottom tray. Draw lines on the side panels of the cabinet to represent the bottom edges of the slide supports. Make sure the lines are level and are perpendicular to the cabinet front. Cut the slide supports to length from 1 × 2 hardwood stock (or any hardwood ripped to 1½" wide).

Face of support flush with edge of face frame

Mount the supports to the side panels of the cabinet with glue and screws driven through countersunk pilot holes. *Note: Depending on the overhang of the cabinet face frames, you may need thicker support stock to provide sufficient clearance for the trays and slide rails.*

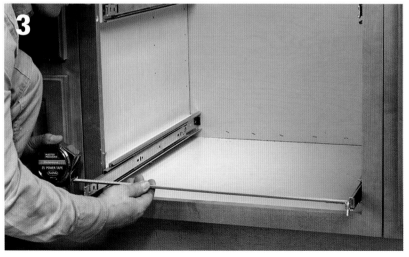

Install the drawer slides flush with the bottom edges of the slide supports using the provided screws. Assemble the two halves of each slide, and then measure between the drawer side pieces (rails) to find the exact width of each tray.
Plan the depth of the trays based on the cabinet depth.

Cut the bottom piece for each tray from ¾" plywood 1½" smaller than the planned width and depth of the finished tray. Rip three ¾"-wide pieces for the sides, front, and back of each tray. Cut the side pieces to length, equal to the depth dimension of the bottom piece. Cut the front and back pieces 1½" longer than the width of the bottom.

Build the trays with glue and 6d finish nails or pneumatic brads. Fasten the sides flush with the bottom face and front and back edges of the bottom piece, and then add the front and back pieces. Sand any rough surfaces, and finish the trays with two or three coats of polyurethane or other durable varnish. If desired, you can stain the trays prior to finishing so they match your cabinets.

Partially mount the drawer slide rails to one of the trays, following the manufacturer's directions. Test-fit the tray in the cabinet and make any necessary adjustments before completely fastening the rails. Mount the slide rails on the remaining trays and install the trays to finish the job.

Pull-out Pantry

You can transform a small walk-in closet into a highly efficient pullout pantry by replacing ordinary shelving with slide-out drawers. This is a great way to customize your kitchen and make it more user-friendly. You can find slide-out drawers for do-it-yourself installation at online sellers. Look for shelves and rollers that are rated to 75 or 100 pounds so you don't have to worry about overload.

There are many options when planning a project such as this. You can purchase shelf rollers that mount to the back of the closet and to the doorframe, or you can purchase shelf rollers that attach to the walls of the pantry. Each requires some modification to the closet structure. This project uses side-mounted rollers. If you have a pantry with sides that are set back from the door to accommodate shelves along the sides as well, you will need to build out the wall surfaces of the side walls to be flush with the door frame. It is best to create a solid wall surface, rather than simply framing the wall. A solid wall surface prevents items from falling off shelves. Closet pantries come in many shapes and sizes. The pantry we are remodeling is a 24 × 24 pantry with only a slight setback and shelves only along the back.

Tools & Materials ▸

Work gloves	Shelves
Eye protection	Lumber
Stud finder	(1 × 4, 2 × 4, lattice)
Tape measure	Roller hardware
Level	Wood or drywall screws
Table saw	Paint (optional)
Drill	

A group of pull-out pantry trays dramatically increases the storage capabilities of the former closet.

How to Install a Pullout Pantry

1

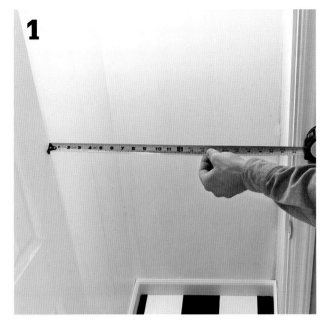

Measure the width of the door opening. Make sure to measure at more than one location in case the door opening is not true. Use the smallest measurement to order or make the sliding shelves. Use a stud finder to locate the studs on the side walls. Mark the locations of the studs.

2

Mark hardware locations. First, measure the setback of the wall from the doorframe on each side. Be sure to include the doorstop trim in your measurement. This depth equals the thickness of the spacers you will need for mounting the roller hardware. Mark the locations of each shelf on the side walls. Use a carpenter's level or laser level to make sure your shelf marks are level.

3

Install spacer blocks. Cut the spacers to length from material of the appropriate thickness, as determined by your measurements. If you have a table saw you can rip spacers to thickness, otherwise use combinations of 1 × 4, 2 × 4, and lattice to achieve the desired depth. Mount the spacers to the studs, centered over the shelf height lines. Paint the spacers, if desired.

4

Assemble and install the shelf slides. Check for level using a carpenter's level or torpedo level. Install the shelves on the rollers. Cut the shelves to size if you're making your own. Finish as desired and mount to the slides.

Vertical Cabinet Dividers

Most kitchen cabinets are based on a one-box-fits-all design, and this works fine for much of the stuff we need to store there. But some things just aren't convenient to store on a horizontal shelf; namely large, flat items like platters, party trays, cutting boards, and baking sheets. These common kitchen products end up getting loaded onto shelves in heavy stacks, and when you need an item it's inevitably near the bottom of the stack.

Vertical cabinet dividers solve this common problem by letting you stow the big flat stuff on their edges, making for easy retrieval of items. You can custom fit the dividers for any wall or base cabinet. One of the best places to use dividers is in over-the-fridge cabinets, which are short and wide and tend to be a good fit for sheets and platters without wasting space. If this space is too high or too cumbersome to reach up and over the fridge, consider using the space above or below a fixed shelf in a full-height cabinet.

The following steps show an adjustable method that allows you to move dividers as needed to accommodate new storage items. The option shown here includes fixed dividers but retains a little more headroom in the cabinet than with the adjustable system. If necessary, a fixed divider can be moved by unscrewing and refastening its slotted cleats.

Tools & Materials ▸

Work gloves
Eye protection
Circular saw
Straightedge guide
Router and $5/16$"
    straight bit
Drill
T-square
Clamps

Tape measure
$3/8$" MDF
$1/4$" plywood
Wood screws or coarse-
    thread drywall screws
1×2 or 2×2 cleats
    (optional)
Pencil

Vertical storage of flat pieces means less wasted cabinet space and no more sorting through stacks when retrieving or replacing an item.

How to Install Vertical Dividers

Cut two MDF panels to fit the inside dimensions of the top and bottom of the cabinet. On one of the pieces, mark the locations of the divider slots using any spacing you like. *Note: With traditional face-frame cabinets, you may need extra MDF pieces or lumber spacers behind the slotted piece so that the slots extend below the face-frame overhang.*

Clamp the MDF pieces to a bench with their faces up and their edges aligned. Using a router and a straightedge guide, mill a ⁵⁄₁₆"-wide × ³⁄₁₆"-deep groove into both pieces at each slot location. If the cabinet has a center partition (middle stile), cut the pieces in half so you'll be able to fit them into the cabinet.

Install the top and bottom pieces into the cabinet so the slots are aligned. Fasten the top piece in place with screws. Measure vertically between the slot bottoms, then cut the divider panels ¹⁄₁₆" shorter than this dimension. Slide the panels into place at the desired spacing.

Variation: For a cabinet with a deeply overhanging face frame, you can save headroom by using slotted 1 × 2 or 2 × 2 cleats to hold the panels instead of solid top and bottom pieces. Mill the cleats with a router and fasten them to the cabinet with screws.

Dish Rack

The holding capacity and clean vertical lines of this dish rack could easily make it a beloved fixture in your kitchen. The efficient, open design lets air circulate to dry mugs, bowls, and plates more efficiently than most in-the-sink types of racks. The rack is handsome enough to double as a display rack to simultaneously store and showcase your dinnerware. Even though it has a small footprint, the rack lets you dry or store up to 20 full-size dinner plates plus cups or glasses. The tall dowels in the back of the rack are removable so you can rearrange them to accommodate large or unusually shaped dishes. The sides have a slight backward slant that gives you easier access to the dishes. This slant requires cutting a diagonal line from the top to the bottom.

This compact drying rack is handsome enough to do double duty as a display rack.

Tools, Materials & Cutting List ▸

Tools

Work gloves
Eye protection
Circular saw
Clamps
Drill with bits
Finish sander
Combination square
Tape measure

Materials

Oak stop molding
Oak Lumber (1 × 2, 1 × 6, 1 × 10)
⅜"-dia. oak doweling
Waterproof wood glue
Wood screws (#8 × 1⅝")
4d finish nails
⅜"-dia. flat oak plugs
Rubber feet (4, optional)
Finishing materials

Key	Part	Dimension
A	(2) Side	¾ × 9¼ × 17" oak
B	(1) Back	¾ × 5½ × 20" oak
C	(2) Shelf front/back	¾ × ¾ × 17" molding
D	(1) Shelf divider	¾ × ¾ × 18½" molding
E	(2) Shelf end	¾ × ¾ × 2¼" molding
F	(2) Rail	¾ × 1½ × 20" oak
G	(19) Back dowel	⅜"-dia. × 10½" dowel
H	(19) Front dowel	⅜"-dia. × 1⅝" dowel

How to Build a Dish Rack

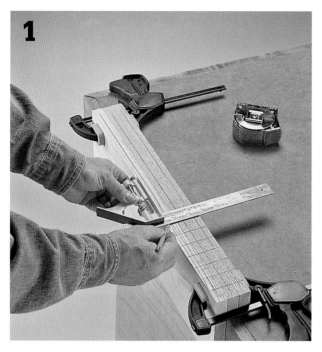

Cut the two rails and the back to size and clamp them together so you can mark the dowel locations on all three parts at the same time. Use a combination square as a guide for drawing the dowel reference lines. Cut the shelf parts to size.

Assemble them with glue and finish nails. Also cut the rack sides to size. Assemble the sides to the back and rails with glue and counterbored screws and then attach the shelf unit between the sides.

Cut the long back dowels to length, slightly longer than the distance from the bottom of the back panel to the lower rail. Insert one end of each dowel into a hole in the back panel and press it up until the bottom end clears the top of the rail. Position the bottom ends over the rail holes and let them drop in.

Glue the dowels into the holes in the front rail, and then fasten the front rail between the sides using glue and counterbored screws. Plug all screw holes, sand, and finish with a water-resistant top coat, such as polyurethane.

Pantry Shelf

Most pantries are great for storing kitchen supplies or appliances that you don't use every day. However, if your pantry itself is poorly organized and inconvenient to use, it winds up as wasted space in your home. To get the most from your pantry, we devised a shelving unit that provides maximum vertical storage capacity. Standing 84" high, the shelf features three solid shelves for storing heavy goods and two adjustable shelves to fit large or awkward items.

You can use this project as a freestanding unit against a wall or as a divider within a larger pantry. The open construction also means you can identify what you have on hand at a glance.

Included in the instructions is a simple option for converting an adjustable shelf into a rack that is perfect for stable storage of wine, soda, or other bottled liquids.

This adjustable shelving unit provides the versatility needed to organize your pantry.

Tools, Materials & Cutting List ▸

Tools

Work gloves
Eye protection
Circular saw
Straightedge
Drill with bits
Finish sander
Nail set
Hammer
Masking tape
Framing Square
Clamps
Perforated hardboard
Wood mallet

Materials

1 × 4" × 8 ft. pine (14)
¾ × ¾" × 6 ft. pine stop
    molding (2)
Wood glue
Wood screws (#6 × 1¼", 1¾",
    #8 × 1⅝")
¼" shelf pins (8)
⅜"-dia. wood plugs
Finishing materials
4d finish nails

Key	Part	Dimension
A	(6) Side slat	¾ × 3½ × 84" pine
B	(9) Fixed-shelf slat	¾ × 3½ × 30½" pine
C	(6) Fixed-shelf face	¾ × 3½ × 30½" pine
D	(6) Fixed-shelf end	¾ × 3½ × 10½" pine
E	(6) Fixed-shelf stretcher	¾ × 3½ × 10½" pine
F	(6) Adjustable shelf slat	¾ × 3½ × 30⅜" pine
G	(4) Adjustable shelf stretcher	¾ × 3½" × 12" pine
H	(10) Wine-shelf cleat	¾ × 3¾" × 12" pine

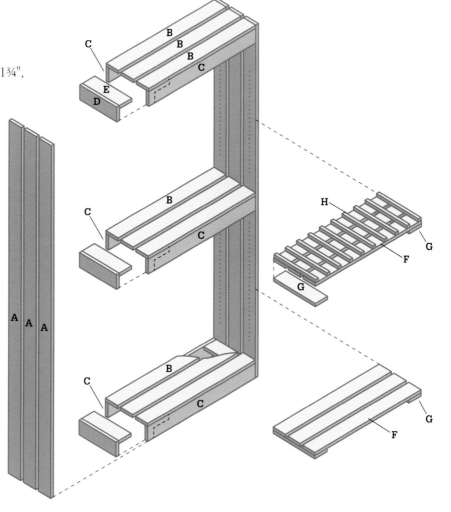

How to Build a Pantry Shelf

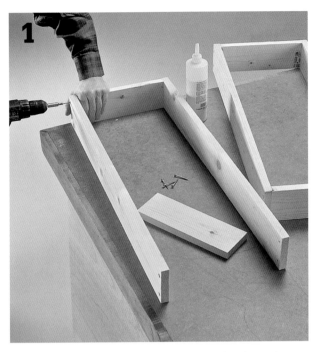

Begin assembling the fixed shelves by cutting the ends and faces to size, and then joining them with glue and counterbored screws. Check with a framing square to make sure the frames you're assembling are square.

Add the stretchers to the tops of the fixed shelf frames. In addition to strengthening the fixed shelf units, the stretchers provide nailing or screwing surfaces for attaching the shelf slats.

Cut the fixed-shelf slats to length, sand them, and attach them to the fixed shelf frames by driving 1¼" screws up through counterbored pilot holes in the stretchers and into the bottom of the slats. Keep your spacing even and make sure the slats do not overhang the frame ends.

Assembly Tips ▶

1. Buy or make wood plugs to fill counterbored screw holes. Building centers usually carry a variety of plug types, sizes, and styles. To cut your own, you can use either a special-purpose plug-cutting tool or a small hole saw that mounts to your power drill. The diameter of the plug must match the counterbore.

2. You will find it helpful to clamp parts during the assembly process. Clamping will hold glued and squared parts securely in place until you permanently fasten them with screws. Large or awkward assemblies are more manageable with the help of a few clamps.

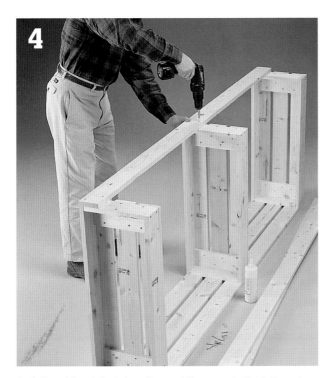

4

Cut the side slats to length, sand them, and attach them to the outside of the fixed shelf units with glue and counterbored wood screws. Make sure the spacing is correct and that all joints are square

5

Drill adjustable shelf peg holes in the side slats. To ensure good results, make a drilling template from a piece of perforated hardboard. Stick a piece of masking tape to a twist bit that's the same diameter as your shelf pins, ½" away from the top. Use the tape as a drilling depth gauge.

6

Build an adjustable shelf to support a wine rack, using a 2½" wide spacer to set the distances separating the wine shelf cleats. Attach the cleats to the shelf with glue and 4d finish nails. Make the other adjustable shelf.

7

Insert shelf pins and install the adjustable shelves. Fill screw-hole counterbores with wood plugs, trim flush, and sand. Finish the shelf as desired. Because it is for indoor use you may leave it unfinished for a rustic look if you prefer.

Pine Pantry

This compact pantry cabinet is ideal for keeping your kitchen organized and efficient. It features a convenient turntable shelf, or lazy Susan, on the inside of the cabinet for easy access to canned foods. A swing-out shelf assembly lets you get the most from the pantry's space. The roominess allows you to store most of your nonrefrigerated food items.

But the best feature of the pantry is its appearance. The rugged beauty of the cabinet hides its simplicity. For such an impressive-looking project, it is remarkably easy to build. Even if you don't have a traditional pantry in your home, you can have a convenient, attractive storage center.

Turn a remote corner or closet into a kitchen pantry with this charming pine cabinet.

Tools, Materials & Cutting List ▸

Tools
Work gloves
Eye protection
Wood glue
Drill with bits
Pencil
Hammer
Compass
Jigsaw
Sand paper
Tape measure

Materials
Wood screws (#6 × 1¼",
    1½", 2")
Finish nails (2d, 4d, 6d)
16-ga. × 1" wire nails
Lazy Susan hardware
Cabinet handles
3 × 3" butt hinges (2)
3 × 3" brass hinges (2)
Cabinet door hinges (4)
¾" cove molding
⅜ × 1¼" stop molding
Pine Lumber (1 × 10,
    1 × 6, 1 × 3, 1 × 4,
    1 × 2, 1 × 8)
Plywood (¼", ¾")
Finishing materials

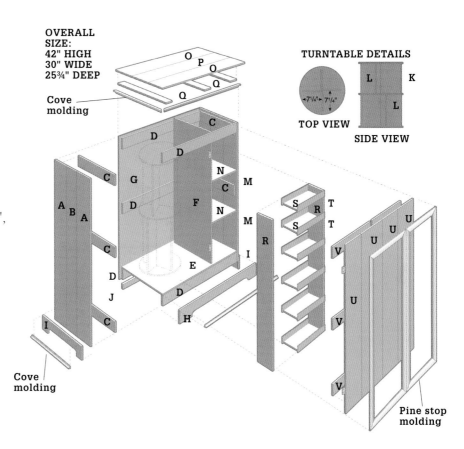

OVERALL
SIZE:
42" HIGH
30" WIDE
25¾" DEEP

Cove molding

TURNTABLE DETAILS

TOP VIEW

SIDE VIEW

Cove molding

Pine stop molding

Key	Part	Dimension
A	(4) Side board	¾ × 9¼ × 39¼" pine
B	(2) Middle board	¾ × 5½ × 39¼" pine
C	(6) Panel cleat	¾ × 2½ × 22½" pine
D	(5) Stretcher	¾ × 2½ × 26½" pine
E	(1) Floor	¾ × 24 × 26½" plywood
F	(1) Divider	¾ × 22½ × 36" plywood
G	(1) Back	¼ × 28 × 39¼" plywood
H	(1) Base front	¾ × 3½ × 29½" pine
I	(2) Base side	¾ × 3½ × 24¼" pine
J	(1) Base back	¾ × 1½ × 28" pine
K	(3) Turntable shelf	¾ × 16"-dia. plywood

Key	Part	Dimension
L	(8) Supports	¾ × 7¼ × 12" pine
N	(2) Fixed shelf	¾ × 9 × 23" plywood
O	(2) Top board	¾ × 9¼ × 30" pine
P	(1) Middle board	¾ × 7¼ × 30" pine
Q	(3) Top cleat	¾ × 2½ × 22¼" pine
R	(2) Swing-out end	¾ × 6 × 32" pine
S	(6) Swing-out shelf	¾ × 6 × 10" pine
T	(12) Swing-out side	¼ × 2 × 11½" plywood
U	(4) Door board	¾ × 6⅞ × 35" pine
V	(6) Door cleat	¾ × 2½ × 11" pine

How to Build a Pine Pantry

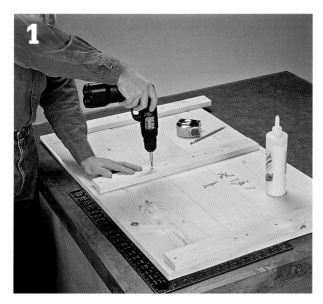

Make the cabinet sides. Cut the side boards, middle boards, and panel cleats to length. Position a middle board between two side boards and set a panel cleat flat across the boards so the bottom edge of the cleat is flush with the bottom edges of the boards. Fasten the cleat to the boards with glue and 1¼" wood screws. Attach the next panel cleat to the boards so its top edge is 21½" up from the bottom edge of the first cleat. Make both sides.

Attach the sides. Cut the side stretchers to length and connect the cabinet sides by attaching the stretchers to the ends of the panel cleats. Position bottom stretchers at the front and back of the cabinet. The back stretcher is flush with the tops and bottoms of the panel cleats, and the front stretcher is flush with the top edges of the cabinet sides. Fasten with glue and 1½" wood screws. Attach the remaining stretcher at the back of the cabinet. Attach the floor.

Attach the divider. Cut the divider and shelf cleats to size. Draw a reference line across the floor from front to back, 9" from the right cabinet side. Mark shelf cleat position lines on the right cabinet side, 10" and 20¾" up from the cabinet floor. Draw corresponding lines on the divider. Use glue and 1¼" wood screws to fasten the shelf cleats to the divider and side. Insert the divider into the cabinet and fasten with glue and 6d finish nails driven into pilot holes.

Attach the back. Cut the back to size and position it on the cabinet. Drive a few 1" wire nails through the back and into one side panel. Measure across opposite corners to check if the cabinet is square and adjust of necessary. When the diagonal measurements are equal, complete the nailing of the back to the stretchers and the remaining side panel. Make the base platform and attach to the cabinet.

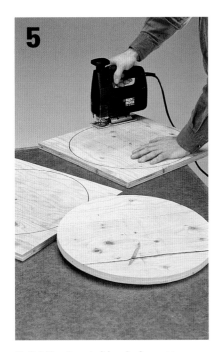

5

Build the turntable shelves. Use a compass to draw 16"-dia. circle and mark plywood for cutting out the three turntable shelves. Cut the shelves to shape with a jigsaw, and sand the cuts smooth.

6

Make the turntable supports. Cut the turntable supports to length and attach pairs of turntable supports at right angles with glue and 1½" wood screws. Fasten the turntable shelves to the turntable supports with glue and 1½" wood screws. Attach Lazy Susan hardware to the bottom turntable shelf.

7

Build the swing-out rack. Cut the swing-out shelves, swing-out ends, and swing-out sides to size. Sand the parts smooth. Attach the shelf edges to the swing-out ends with glue and 1½" wood screws. Attach the swing-out shelf sides on the edges of the shelves with glue and 4d finish nails.

8

Make the top and doors. Cut the boards to size. For the top, attach cleats to the undersides of the top slats and then frame with cove molding. For the doors, attach three cleats to the back sides and then apply a decorative frame on the fronts made from stop molding.

9

Assemble the pantry. Attach two evenly spaced 3 × 3" butt hinges to the edge of the swing-out rack. Mount the rack to the divider using ¼"-thick spacers between the rack and divider. Install the turntable assembly on the floor of the pantry. Attach hinges and handles to the doors. Mount the doors to the cabinet sides. Apply finish as desired.

Pull-down Shelves

A pull-down shelf makes wall cabinets more user-friendly by bringing all the contents down to eye level. Because of the space taken up by the mechanism and the shelf boxes, this is not a good project for a narrow cabinet.

Before you begin this project, hold each swing arm assembly against the inside face of the cabinet side and make sure both arms will clear the door hinge and the cabinet face frame. If the arms do not clear, add custom wood spacers of plywood or solid lumber that are at least as large as the swing arm mounting plates.

Follow the manufacturer's specifications for the box dimensions, which will be based on the size of your cabinet. If the boxes are bare wood, lightly sand the edges and finish all sides with a highly washable paint or a clear varnish, such as polyurethane. For melamine-coated board, cover the cut edges with melamine tape to keep water from damaging the wood core.

Note: The springs that help raise the arms are strong and may make it difficult to lower empty shelves. When the shelves are loaded, the weight of the items makes it easier to move the shelf.

Tools & Materials ▸

Work gloves	Finishing materials
Eye protection	Swing-up shelf kit
Tape measure	& hardware (see
Pencil	Resources, page 234)
Drill	#8 panhead screws
Awl	Coarse-thread wallboard
Circular saw	screws
Allen wrench	Lumber for custom
½" MDF	spacers

A pull-down shelf is mounted in an upper wall cabinet, and can be drawn out of the cabinet and lowered so the user can reach the contents more easily.

How to Install a Pull-down Shelf

Use the shelf manufacturer's paper template to determine the general positions of the swing arms, then fasten the wood spacers to the inside faces of the cabinets with coarse-thread wallboard screws. The screws should not go completely through the cabinet side.

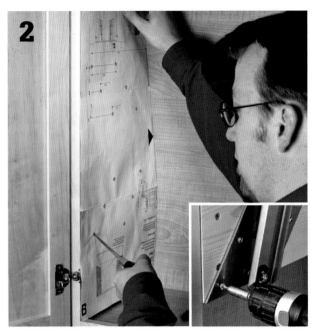

Use the template as a reference for marking the location of the swing arm mounting plates with a scratch awl. Drill a pilot hole at each mark. Fasten the swing arms to the custom spacers or cabinet sides with #8 panhead screws (inset). The screws should not go completely through the cabinet side.

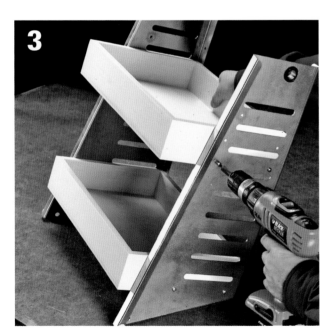

Build two shelf boxes from ½" MDF. Install the boxes between the sides of the shelf unit using the predrilled holes in the side pieces. Secure the boxes with #8 panhead screws. Because the lower box can be installed in only one position, install it first. Then find the desired position for the upper box and secure it in place. Slide the lower handle through the holes in the side pieces.

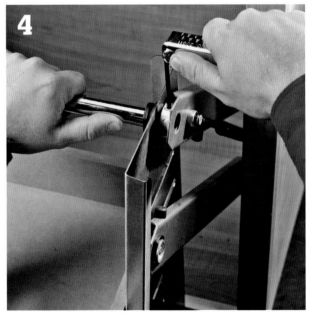

Cut the upper handle to length. With the assistance of a helper, position the box unit in front of the cabinet, rotate the lower arms downward, and secure them to the side pieces using the bolts, washers, and nuts provided. Insert the top handle. Lower the upper arms one at a time and insert the handle end into the arm. Secure the handle with the two setscrews in each arm using an Allen wrench.

Bathrooms

Boat builders would make great bathroom designers: they're experts at shoehorning loads of stuff into tiny spaces while making everything look good and function smoothly. When it comes to streamlining and organizing your own bathroom, it pays to think like a boat builder: Where can you add storage without encroaching on floor space? Are there opportunities for using dual-purpose features, such as a freestanding shelf unit that acts as a partition wall? How can you arrange supplies more neatly and efficiently?

Storage systems in the bathroom range from the quick and simple, like towel hooks and shower caddies, to the clever and custom, like the recessed wall cabinet on page 66. Another basic idea that works particularly well in bathrooms is to blend storage and display: keeping everyday supplies like cotton balls and soaps in attractive containers and setting them out on the vanity top or lining them up on shallow shelves. Some essentials can even go outside of the bathroom, such as towels kept in a cabinet that's tucked into a corner of an adjacent hallway. With a keen eye and a little creative brainstorming, even the most space-challenged bathrooms can yield a surprising number of storage opportunities.

In this chapter
- Storage Strategies
- Full-height Medicine Cabinet
- Wall-hung Bath Cabinet
- Towel Towers
- Glass Shelves

Storage Strategies

A well-planned bathroom blurs the line between utility space and living space; it is both functional and aesthetically pleasing at the same time. The secret to finding the right balance is to first determine what each bathroom really needs to serve its purpose, then to look for storage solutions that meet those needs while complementing the overall scheme.

A busy family bathroom may have very different requirements from a half bath used primarily by guests. In the former, it's OK to store toiletries and medicines out in the open and to hang wet towels on the back of the bathroom door. In the latter, only essential powder room supplies are appropriate: soaps, hand towels, lotions, tissues, etc. Homes with a single bathroom present a bigger challenge, but this can be met with a combination of concealed storage and practical but attractive accessories. Consider the following options and strategies to find the best plan for your private or public retreats.

An assortment of economical bathroom storage units and accessories can be found at most neighborhood home centers. For more distinctive pieces, shop online, where you can find a full range of styles and designs from classic American to modern.

Bathroom Storage Options

For sheer quantity of storage space in any bathroom, you can't beat a traditional vanity cabinet or a built-in linen closet. They're ideal for storing everything you don't want out in the open and for keeping towels and paper products clean and dry. The tips on page 64 can help you make the most of these workhorse storage units. If you're lacking a cabinet or closet, perhaps you can find room for a freestanding storage cabinet, such as an armoire or a small chest of drawers.

The medicine cabinet is another reliable standard, ideally sized and located for storing the jumble of small bathroom items you need every day. Recessed cabinets with mirrors are a prime example of efficient bathroom storage: the cabinet box uses the free space between wall studs, while the mirror provides an essential bathroom feature—all with virtually no loss of room space. As an alternative, wall-mounted medicine cabinets with solid-wood doors offer space-efficient concealed storage in a furniture-quality unit. Deeper wall cabinets can hold bulkier items like towels and toilet paper rolls without taking up floor space.

Shelves can be a real boon to a bathroom storage plan because they can take almost any form and fit where other units won't. A wall-length ledge capping a tall wainscot of paneling or wallpaper provides a natural visual transition and is great for holding glass jars, perfume bottles, and display items. Small glass shelves above a sink work well in lieu of a medicine cabinet or vanity drawers. For a nice custom shelving unit, you can build a niche inside a wall-stud cavity and finish it with tile or another washable surface. And don't forget the empty wall space above the toilet: it can be filled with custom wall-to-wall shelves or a freestanding or wall-mounted étagère.

Hardworking bathrooms can never have too many hooks or towel bars. Make sure you have them within arm's reach of the tub or shower, as well as next to each sink. In addition to holding wet towels, hooks are great for hanging bathrobes and clothes, shower bags, and totes filled with extra bath supplies. Empty wall spaces can double your towel storage when bars are mounted with one above the other (you can also find double bars that hang two towels in single file). If you'd rather not use up wall space with standard hooks or bars, you can substitute with a floor-standing towel tree or, for a creative touch, a conventional coat tree. And keep in mind that hooks and some bars can go almost anywhere—on furniture pieces, at the front or sides of vanity cabinets, on door and window trim, or on the bathroom door itself.

To help guests feel comfortable in a shared bathroom, make sure there are hand towels hanging next to the sink, and try to keep wet bath towels away from the toilet and sink areas.

Wall-mounted bath cabinets can include an open shelf below for display-worthy items, or even a towel bar or hooks for extra linen storage.

The right furniture piece can add warmth and a casual elegance to a bathroom décor. In some cases, it can be converted for custom duty, as with this dresser that has become a vanity cabinet.

This towel rack with shelf helps manage the bathroom's linen storage. Clean towels and washcloths are stowed above while used towels hang out to dry below.

Neatly carved out of a wall cavity, a shelving niche makes a beauty of a built-in. You can finish the sides and back of the recess with drywall and tile, paint, or thin wood paneling.

Taming Toiletries & Other Bathroom Essentials

Bathrooms are natural clutter zones, mostly due to the constant influx and turnover of personal products and other supplies. Small and numerous as they are, these items are much more manageable if they're stored in an organized fashion. Here are some suggestions for keeping track of your bathroom basics:

TOILETRIES

For general hygiene products, follow the same point of use and frequency of use rules applied to kitchen tools: arrange the everyday stuff right where you use it, near the sink or in upper drawers of a vanity cabinet. Transferring supplies like cotton swabs and makeup sponges to attractive glass containers lets you keep them out in the open without creating a cluttered look (uniform containers are easier on the eye than busy product packaging). Store extra supplies in their packages in one location under the sink or in a nearby closet so you'll know where to go for refills. A matching set of vanity accessories—soap dish, toothbrush holder, cups, etc.—offers a unified look and helps minimize visual clutter in shared baths.

Maintain order inside vanity drawers by storing items by category in divided trays or drawer organizers. This prevents the inevitable migration of small things like hair ties and nail files to the back of the drawer. Backup supplies of shampoos, lotions, and other bulky items are best kept in plastic bins that you can easily slide in and out of cabinets or closet shelves. Group items by theme so you can readily find what you need.

MAKEUP & MEDICINES

Besides being major sources of bathroom clutter, makeup and medicines have one important thing in common: they don't last forever. It's pretty obvious when old makeup becomes funky or gloppy, while expired medicines may simply not work like they should. Both call for ruthless periodic culling of the old stuff. To manage the rest, again look to plastic bins, trays, and shelf or drawer organizers, and group like items for easy retrieval. Store frequent-use items close at hand. Stash everything else out of the way while following an organized plan. If you have young children or babies, it helps to store each child's medicines in one place, along with dosage charts and other care information.

An organizer tray, like those made for office supplies, keeps a vanity drawer from turning into a junk heap.

Plastic lidded containers are great for storing occasional-use medicines, first aid supplies, and seasonal products. Arrange items by category and label each bin for quick identification.

SHOWER & BATH SUPPLIES

Hair products and bath supplies tend to linger long past their prime in most bathrooms, along with travel-size bottles of shampoo, miniature soaps, and mystery gels that always find a way into luggage at the end of hotel visits. Either throw this stuff out or force yourself to use it before replacing bottles of your regular products. Cutting clutter in the bathing area helps keep bathtub ledges and shower shelves clean and mildew free. Tight shower spaces can benefit from a simple wire shower caddy or a built-in niche.

Shower storage solutions: A built-in niche (left) or a shower caddy (right) keep shampoos and soaps off of the tub rim without cutting into useable shower space.

Family Bath ▶

Keep a well-ventilated laundry basket in the bottom of a linen closet or other inconspicuous spot and designate it for used towels and washcloths only. This keeps the wet stuff out of the regular laundry collection and helps prevent mildew between laundry days.

Full-height Medicine Cabinet

A classic medicine chest is a great storage solution for several reasons. First, it keeps your stuff right where you need it, near the sink. Second, its multiple shallow shelves store small items in plain view, so there's no digging around for everyday necessities. Built-in medicine cabinets are recessed into the wall, minimizing the use of precious room space. And finally, most medicine chests serve a dual purpose in the bathroom by having mirrored doors.

Indeed, the basic medicine chest design leaves little room for improvement. That's why the bathroom cabinet in this project takes the same great features and simply makes more of them. This built-in cabinet has a 3½"-deep storage space yet projects only ¾" from the wall (not counting the overhead crown molding). Inside, it's loaded with adjustable shelves, so it can hold not only prescription bottles and toiletries, but also taller things like shampoo bottles and cleaning supplies. And the cabinet's door is tall enough to accommodate a full-length mirror—a great convenience feature for any bathroom.

The box of this medicine cabinet is sized to fit into a standard 14½"-wide space between wall studs. With the drywall cut away, the box slips into place and mounts directly to the studs. Then you trim out the cabinet to fit the style of your bathroom. The traditional molding treatment shown here is only one way to do it; you can add any type of molding and extras you like using the same techniques. Another option is to build a similar cabinet that mounts to the surface of the wall, as shown in the Variation on page 71. With this design, you're not limited by the width and depth of a stud cavity, but the cabinet does occupy a small amount of floor space.

Using less than two feet of wall space, this built-in cabinet offers more than enough room for a household's medicines, toiletries, and backup bathroom supplies.

Tools & Materials ▸

Tools
Work gloves
Eye protection
Tape measure
Circular saw
Miter Saw
Drill/driver
Clamps
Chisel
Mallet
Drywall saw
Putty knife
Level
Drill guide
Paint Brush
Caulk Gun

Materials
AC plywood (¼", ¾")
Poplar (1 × 4, 1 ×6)
Shims
Pegboard
Shelf pins
Door catch
Finish nails (1½, 2¼")
Construction adhesive
Mirror (approx. 10 × 48")
Wood putty
Finishing materials

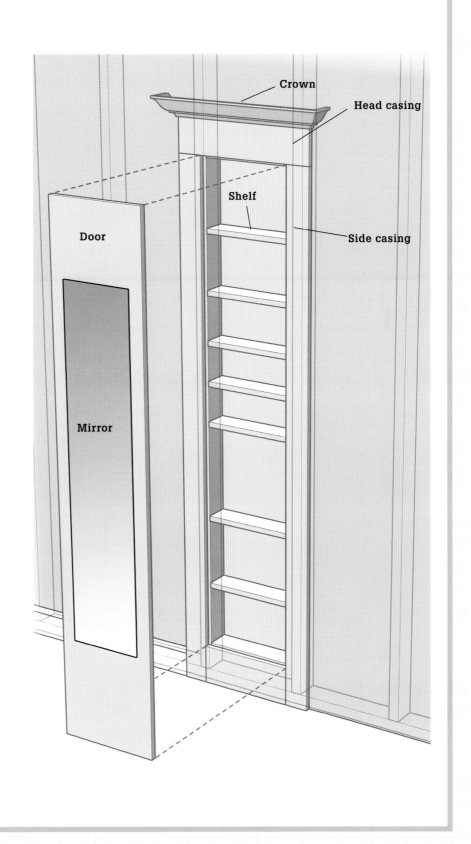

Crown
Head casing
Shelf
Door
Side casing
Mirror

How to Install a Full-height Cabinet

Determine the overall height of the finished cabinet (with trim), then subtract the height of the trim assembly above the door. Add ¼" to find the height of the cabinet box. Measure up from the floor and draw a level at the installed box height between two wall studs where the cabinet will go.

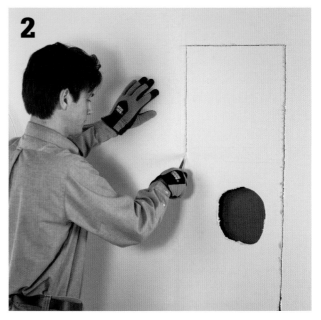

Cut one or more exploratory holes in the drywall between the host studs, then examine the stud cavity to make sure that no electrical cables, plumbing pipes, or other elements intersect the cavity. Cut out the drywall between the studs, up to the level line.

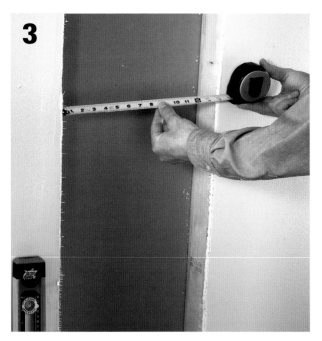

Measure between the studs to determine the overall width of the cabinet box. *Tip: If the studs aren't plumb, leave some extra room for adjusting the cabinet when you install it (see step 8, on page 69).*

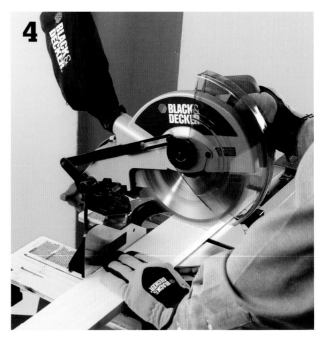

Cut the two side pieces for the cabinet box to length, 1½" shorter than the floor-to-top dimension from step 1. Cut the top piece, middle shelf, and bottom shelf 1½" shorter than the overall cabinet width. Cut the adjustable shelves ³⁄₁₆" shorter than the fixed shelves. Cut the back panel equal to the overall width of the cabinet and the same length as the sides.

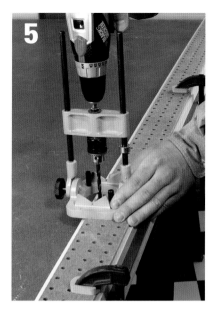

Drill holes into the box sides for the adjustable shelf pins using pegboard with ¼" holes as a drilling guide. Align the pegboard so the hole pairs are evenly spaced across each side piece, and drill the holes to a depth of ⅝" using a stop collar on the bit. Make sure the hole pairs are matched on both pieces so the shelves will hang level.

Assemble the cabinet box by fastening the sides over the ends of the top and bottom and middle shelves using glue and 2" screws. Position the bottom shelf so its top face is 4½" from the ends of the sides. Position the top piece flush with the top ends of the sides, and position the middle shelf roughly halfway in between.

Fasten the back panel to the assembly with 1" screws. Align the box sides and top with the panel edges as you work to ensure the assembly is square. Prime all sides of the box, including the back, and then add two top coats of paint to the box interior and front edges of the side pieces.

Set the box into place between the wall studs and check it for plumb. Use cedar shims to fill any gaps along the studs and to adjust for plumb. Fasten the box sides to the studs with 2" screws so the front edges of the sides are flush with the surface of the drywall.

(continued)

9

Cut, prime, and install the 1 × 4 side trim and 1 × 6 base trim with 2¼" finish nails, overlapping the sides of the box by ¼". Add the bead and head trim over the ends of the side trim. Install the crown molding over the head trim with 1½" finish nails, mitering the corners and adding return pieces back to the wall. Measure the opening created by the trim pieces and cut the door panel ⅛" narrower and shorter than the opening.

10

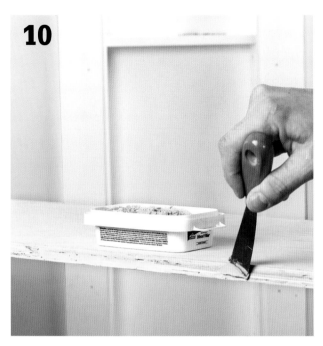

Fill any voids in the panel edges with wood putty or auto body filler, then sand the panel smooth and prime and paint the panel. Paint the cabinet trim, and fill and paint over the screw heads inside the cabinet box.

11

Mount the door to the side trim with three small butt hinges or a single piano hinge. Mortise-in butt hinges for a flush fit. Install a drawer pull or knob, then add a magnetic door catch onto the door and cabinet box side.

12

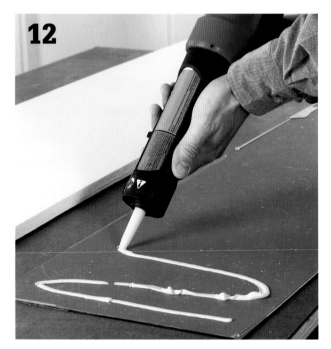

Have the mirror cut to the desired size by a glass dealer. Secure the mirror to the front of the door panel with a recommended adhesive (you can remove the door if you used butt hinges). If desired, add trim around the edges of the mirror. Install the adjustable shelves.

Variation: Surface-mount Cabinet ▶

This surface-mount cabinet is a freestanding unit that you secure to the wall for stability. You can use this design if a recessed cabinet is impractical or undesirable for your situation. The basic construction steps are similar to those of the recessed unit:

1. Assemble the cabinet box with a fixed top, middle shelf, bottom shelf, and back panel. If you want a deeper cabinet, you can substitute 1 × 6 lumber for the box sides, top, and shelves.

2. Add 1 × 2 side trim pieces to the front of the box, then add a 1 × 4 head trim piece and a 1 × 6 base trim piece between the side trim. Cut the door to fit between the side, head, and base trim pieces.

3. Add the crown molding, then prime and paint all parts. Hang the door with hinges secured to the side trim.

4. Secure the cabinet to a wall stud with screws driven through the back panel. Wrap the base of the cabinet with baseboard trim for a built-in look. Add quarter-round molding along the cabinet sides to hide the edges of the back panel and any gapping caused by wall contours.

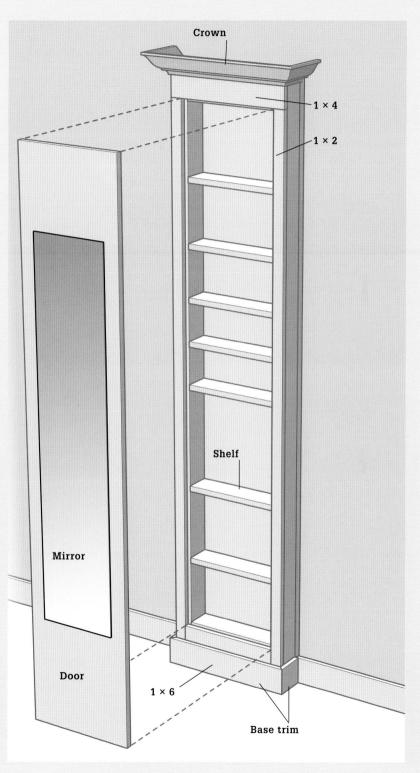

Wall-hung Bath Cabinet

Cabinetry and casework are fundamental to making built-ins and bookcases. This small wall-hung cabinet is not only a convenient storage space, it is also a great project for a beginning carpenter to develop some basic cabinetry skills. It is also extremely inexpensive to make. The entire case, including the top, can be built from an 8-foot-long piece of 1 × 10 wood (you'll need a little extra material for the shelving and the towel rod). The mitered frames applied to the front of the doors give the look and feel of a raised panel door without any of the fuss.

We built the version of the cabinet you see here out of No. 2 and better pine, and then gave it an orangey maple finish. You can choose any lumber you like for this, even sheet stock such as MDF, and apply a clear or a painted finish. For a traditional look, choose a white enamel paint. Be sure to apply several thin coats of polyurethane varnish, especially when installing in a wet area like a bathroom.

Simple styling lets this bathroom wall cabinet fit into just about any bathroom.

Tools, Materials & Cutting List ▸

Tools

Work gloves
Eye protection
Framing square
Tape measure
Combination square
Router, profiling bit
Circular saw or table saw
Jigsaw
Clamps
Hammer
Finish hammer

Needlenose
   pliers
Drill/driver
¾" spade bit
Wood glue
Finishing tools
File
Plastic screw
   insert
   (optional)

Materials

1 × 10" × 8 ft. pine
1 × 8" × 4 ft. pine
Backer board
1 × 2 lumber
¾" Dowel
Screen retainer molding
   (10 lineal ft.)
Door knobs (2)
Touch latches (2)
Hinges (2)
Wood screws
Finish nails (3d, 6d)
Finishing materials

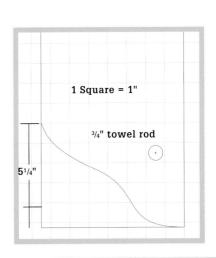

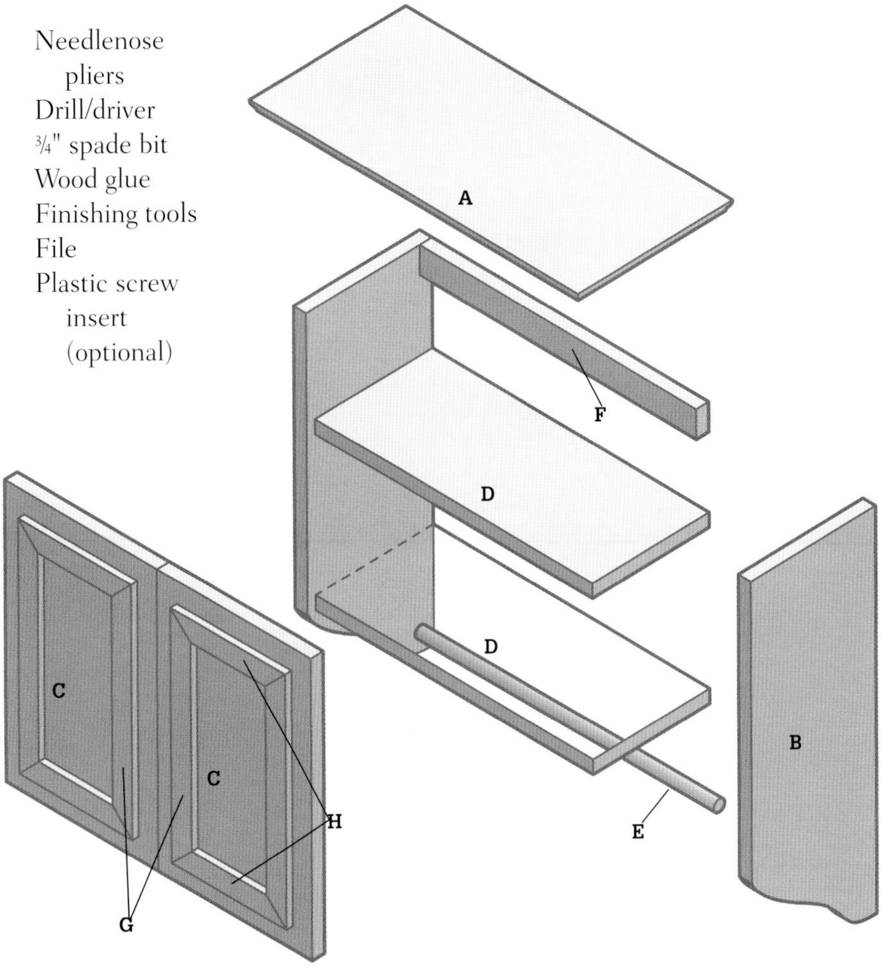

Part	No.	Desc.	Size	Material
A	1	Top	¾ × 9¼ × 19½	1 × 10 pine
B	2	Sides	¾ × 7½ × 20¼	1 × 10 or 1 × 8 pine
C	2	Doors	¾ × 9 × 15	1 × 10 pine
D	2	Shelves	¾ × 7 × 16½	1 × 8 pine
E	1	Towel rod	¾ × 18"	Dowel
F	1	Wall cleat	¾ × 1½ × 16½	1 × 2 pine
G		Door molding (short)	¼ × ¾ × cut to fit	Retainer molding
H		Door molding (long)	¼ × ¾ × cut to fit	Retainer molding

1 Square = 1"

¾" towel rod

5¼"

How to Build a Bath Cabinet

PREPARE THE STOCK

This bathroom cabinet can be made almost entirely from a single 8-foot 1 × 10 using basic tools. (If you buy a 10-footer, you'll have enough stock to make all but the middle shelf, which can easily be made from another piece of wood or even glass.) At your local lumberyard or building center, hand-select a board (pine or another wood; No. 2 or better pine is much cheaper than other types in most areas). Look for a board that's straight and free from defects like large knots or waney (barklike) edges. When you get the board home, trim around ¼" off each end (never trust the factory ends—they're seldom squarely cut).

Cut the top board to 19½". Then cut an ogee profile into the front edge and the side edges using a piloted ogee bit (step 1). Be sure to attach blocking at the back edges to prevent the router bit from turning the corner and cutting into the back edge. If you don't own a router, you can simply hand-sand a roundover in the bottom edges or you can try cutting a chamfer profile with a hand plane (a tricky job, but a good skill to develop).

Next, cut the stock for both doors to length, plus a little bit (cut a piece around 30½" long) and either rip-cut the edges to get a clean surface on both sides or sand them or plane them smooth (step 2). The final width of the material should be 9". Once the stock is prepared, cut the doors to length.

Shape a decorative profile into the top using a router and piloted ogee bit. Do not remove more than ¾" of material along the bottom edges.

Use a table saw, circular saw, plane or sander to get straight, crisp edges on the cabinet door stock.

Cut the stock for the cabinet sides to width (7½") or select a piece of 1 × 8 stock and simply sand the edges. Then enlarge the pattern on page 73 using a photocopier to make a hardboard template of the curved shape. Trace the profile on one side, referencing up from the bottom of the board (step 3).

Clamp the two sides together so the ends and edges all are flush. Then, cut out the profile in both pieces at once using a jigsaw (step 4). Make your cuts just short of the cutting line. When the cut is finished, do not unclamp the ganged sides. Use a sander or a round file to smooth the cuts and remove waste wood exactly up to the cutting lines. An oscillating spindle sander is the best tool here. Another good idea is to mount a drum sander in a drill press. Last, before you

unclamp the sides, locate the centerpoint for drilling the ¾"-dia. dowel hole for the towel rod. Drill the hole with a ¾" spade bit, making sure to slip a backer board underneath the bottom board to prevent tearout when the bit exits the workpiece (step 5).

ASSEMBLE THE CABINET

Assembling your bathroom cabinet is a simple process of gluing, clamping, and nailing. It is worth investing in a couple of 24" bar clamps or pipe clamps if you don't own them already, although another option is to use screws instead of nails to fasten the parts, relying on the screws to provide clamp-like pressure to the glue joints. Only do this if you are painting the cabinet.

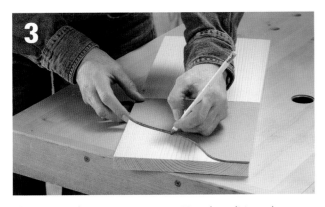

Photocopy the pattern on page 73 and use it to make a hardboard template guide to trace the profile onto the bottom of one cabinet side.

Cut both side profiles at the same time, staying just outside the cutting line so you can sand precisely up to the cutting line.

Still with the sides ganged together, drill a ¾"-dia. hole for the towel rod using a backer board under the bottom side.

(continued)

Press the two shelves and the cleat between the cabinet sides after applying glue to the ends.

Reinforce the glued joints with 6d finish nails driven into pilot holes. Glue the ends of the trowel rod into the holes in the cabinet sides.

Pin the towel rod to the cabinet sides with a finish nail driven through the back edge of each side. Miter the corners of the screen retainer molding.

Nail and glue decorative frames to the door fronts. Hold small finish nails with a needlenose pliers and use a finish hammer (as shown).

Lay the side boards on a flat surface, so they are parallel and on their back edges. Cut the 1 × 2 cleat and the 7"-wide shelves to length (16½"). *Note: The shelves are ½" narrower than the sides to provide clearance for the doors.* Position the cleat and the shelves between the cabinet sides, making sure everything fits squarely. Then apply wood glue to the ends of all three parts and clamp them between the cabinet sides (step 6). Then, clamp the sides with bar clamps and check with a framing square to make sure the sides are square to the shelves. Also make sure the middle shelf is perpendicular to the sides.

Before the glue sets (about 15 minutes), drive three 6d finish nails through the cabinet sides and into each shelf end. Drive a pair of nails into the wall cleat (step 7). It is always a good idea to drill pilot holes for nailing. Insert the towel rod into the holes in the cabinet sides.

Once it is in position, push it inward ½" or so on one side and apply glue to the inside surfaces of the dowel hole. Then press the rod from the other side to reveal about ½" of the hole and apply glue. Push the rod so the ends are flush with the cabinet sides and then drive one 3d finish nail through the back edge of each cabinet side and into the dowel to pin it in place (step 8).

HANG THE DOORS

Cut strips of half-round screen retainer molding to make decorative frames for the front of the cabinet doors. Miter the corners. The frames should be inset 1" or so from the door edges on all sides. Attach the frames to the door fronts with glue and a few finish nails (step 9).

Note: Now is a good time to finish or paint your bathroom cabinet. Be sure to sand all the surfaces well and make sure you remove any dried glue—the stain and finish won't stick to it. We used a gel-type Swedish maple stain on our pine cabinet because it imparts a rich color (it resembles orange shellac) and disguises the fact that pine has very little wood grain. We added three thin coats of wipe-on varnish after the stain dried (step 10).

Hang the cabinet doors with 1½" brushed chrome or nickel butt hinges (step 11). In most cases, you'll need to cut shallow mortises in the cabinet sides and door for the hinges. Center the cabinet top so the overhang is equal on the side and the back is flush with the cabinet back. Attach the top by driving a few finish nails through it and into the top edges of the cabinet sides, as well as into the top edges of the wall cleat (step 12). You're better off not using glue to attach the top.

Install a touch latch at the top of each door opening.

HANG THE CABINET

Locate wall studs in the installation area. Where possible, position the cabinet so it hits two studs. Attach the cabinet with wood screws driven through the wall cleat and into the studs (step 13). If you only have one stud available, drill a ¼" hole through the cleat, as far from a stud location as you can get and still have access. Position the cabinet against the wall and mark the hole onto the wall by inserting a finish nail into the hole. Remove the cabinet and install a plastic screw insert at the hole location. Replace the cabinet and drive a screw so it catches the insert. Then relevel the cabinet and screw the wall cleat to the wall at the stud location. Drill pilot holes in the doors and install door knobs with screws.

Apply your finish or paint the cabinet before you hang the doors and install the cabinet top.

To ensure doors hang flush, use a file to make slight indentations to hinge locations. Hang the doors. Use care to position the doors so the outside edges are flush with the outer faces of the cabinets sides. The tops should be about ⅛" below the top edges of the cabinet sides.

Attach the finished cabinet top to the cabinet sides with 4d finish nails.

Hang the cabinet. If you don't have access to two wall studs, use a plastic screw insert or other hanging hardware in addition to fastening the wall cleat to a wall stud.

Towel Towers

If there's one place in the house that collects everybody's stuff, it's the bathroom. Towels, clothes, cleaning supplies, even laundry. But some fancy design work using a couple of refrigerator wall cabinets and some cool carpentry create a niche spot that can provide a central location for all kinds of different items. Suitable even for small bathrooms, this towel tower also adds texture and color to the space. And another added benefit to this project is the seating provided by the countertop on the cabinet.

The beadboard backing for this project is made with painted ⅜"-thick tongue-and-groove pine, sometimes called carsiding. More advanced carpenters may prefer to make their own custom beadboard from hardwood and give it a custom wood finish.

The base for this project is an over-the-fridge-size wall cabinet (sometimes called a bridge cabinet). At 15" high, it is within the range of comfortable seating heights. But if you prefer a slightly higher seat (and many people do), build a 2 × 4 curb for the cabinet to rest on.

To conceal the seam where the towel tower meets the floor, we trimmed around the base with base shoe trim, mitering the corners. We used the same trim stock to conceal the gap where the seatboard meets the tongue-and-groove paneling. Here, however, we added small miter returns to the ends of the base shoe.

By cleverly repurposing this refrigerator wall cabinet and tongue-and-groove pine, a hum-drum corner has become a comfortable seating and storage area.

Tools, Materials & Cutting List ▶

Tools
Work gloves
Eye protection
Circular saw
Router (with roundover
    and chamfering bit)
Paint brush
Tape measure
Drill/driver
Table saw
Sander
Shims
Tape
4 ft. level

Materials
Scrap wood for backer
2½" deck screws
Pneumatic brad nailer
1 × 6" × 8 ft. pine (2)
4 × 8 tongue-and-groove panels
Crown molding (3 ft.)
½ sheet ¾"-thick MDF
12 ft. quarter-round molding
Towel hooks
Wood screws
2" wallboard screws
Construction adhesive
Pneumatic brads
Wood putty
Primer
Paint

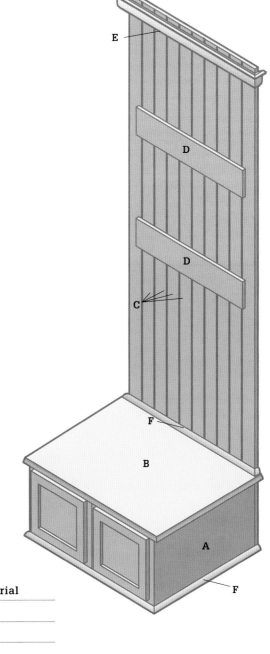

Key	No.	Description	Size	Material
A	1	Over-fridge cabinet	15h × 30w × 24d	
B	1	Seatboard	¾ × 25 × 32*	MDF
C	8	T&G paneling	⅜ × 5½ × 71"**	Pine
D	2	Towel hook backers	¾ × 5½ × 27"	Pine 1 × 6
E	3 lin. ft.	Crown molding	Cut to fit (w/miters)	Pine
F	12 lin. ft.	¼" round molding	Cut to fit	Pine

* Finished size: requires slightly larger board for machining
** Length equals distance from top of seatboard to ceiling minus ½"

How to Build a Towel Tower

INSTALL THE BASE CABINETS

Begin by making the seatboard that tops the refrigerator cabinet. Cut a piece of medium density fiberboard (MDF) so it is 1" wider than the cabinet and a couple of inches longer front-to-back (make it about 26" if using a 24" cabinet as shown here). Mount a piloted ogee or roundover bit (or other profiling bit of your choice) into your router and shape the front and side edges (step 1). You'll probably get a little bit of blow-out at the back edge, which is why it's recommended that you make the workpiece a couple of inches too long. Once you've routed the profiles, trim the back edge so the front overhangs the cabinet by 1". Coat all faces and edges with primer and at least two coats of paint.

Attach the seatboard with screws driven through the mounting strips on the cabinet top and into the underside of the seatboard. The back edge of the seatboard should be flush with the back edge of the cabinet and the overhang should be equal on the sides. Since this cabinet is small, it might be best to clamp the blank in location on the cabinet, then turn the cabinet on its back so you can access the fastener locations more easily (step 2).

Install the cabinet in the project location. Baseboard and any other obstructions should be removed from the project area. Slip shims below and behind the cabinet as needed to make sure it is level and plumb. Attach the cabinet to the wall by driving 2" wallboard screws through the cabinet back at wall stud locations (step 3).

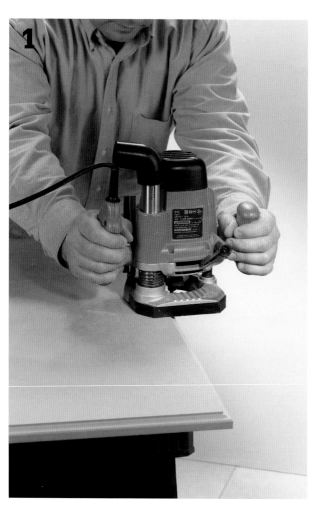

Rout a profile, such as an ogee or roundover, into the sides and front of the seatboard. Use a router table if you have one, otherwise hand-machine it with a piloted profiling bit.

Because these cabinets are so small, it's easier to pregang them together, then flip the assembly upside down to install the seatboard.

INSTALL THE PANELING

The backer board for the towel tower can be made from a number of building materials, while retaining the beadboard appearance that lends a bit of country style to this project. The easiest and cheapest product you can use is beadboard paneling: thin sheet stock that comes in 4 × 8-foot panels. You'll find a wide range of colors, patterns, and qualities in the beadboard sheet stock, including some that are presized to around 42" for installation as wainscoting. The cheapest material has a printed pattern layer laminated over hardboard. The better quality material has hardwood veneer over a plywood or lauan backing. We chose real tongue-and-groove boards made from pine. With actual dimensions of $3/8 × 5\frac{1}{2}$", the carsiding product we used has enough depth to create a convincing profile but is still relatively inexpensive.

Because it is very unlikely that the strips of carsiding will be exactly the same width as your base cabinet once they're installed, you'll need to rip-cut the outside boards to fit the project area (it is better to rip-cut both outer boards an equal amount than to take everything out of one of the boards). To gauge where to make your cuts, assemble enough boards to cover the width of the cabinet and lay them out on a flat surface (step 4). Mark the centerpoint of the middle board and measure out half the distance in each direction. Make ripcut lines at these points.

Drive screws through the back of the cabinet at the marked wall stud locations.

Midpoint

Lay out the tongue-and-groove carsiding boards in a row, with the tongues fitted into grooves. Measure out in one direction (half the width of base cabinets) from a midpoint line in the center board.

(continued)

5

Clamp a straightedge over a tongue-and-groove board, placing a piece of scrap plywood underneath as a backer. Rip-cut the board to the correct thickness for the filler piece.

6

Press the trimmed filler board to the wall, seating it in construction adhesive, at the left edge of the panel area.

Before ripping the boards, trim all of your carsiding stock so it is ¼ to ½" shorter than the distance from the seatboard to the ceiling. Then trim the outer carsiding boards to width using a table saw (make sure you are trimming off the correct edge, be it tongue or groove). If you do not have access to a table saw, use a circular saw and a straightedge cutting guide. With thin stock like this, cutting a scrap wood backer board along with the workpiece will result in a cleaner cut. Make the rip cuts (step 5) and sand the edges if necessary to smooth out the cuts.

Use a 4-foot level to extend plumb lines directly up the wall from the outside edges of the seatboard. Then mark the wall stud locations on the seatboard and ceiling with tape. Begin installing the carsiding on the left side, with the left trimmed board. In most cases, the tongue will be preserved on this board and should be oriented inward (step 6). Apply a heavy bead of construction adhesive to the back of the board and stick it to the wall. If it happens to fall over a wall stud, nail it in place by driving a finish nail (or, preferably, a pneumatic brad) through the tongue at an angle. The nails should be countersunk enough that they do not obstruct the groove of the adjoining board.

Continue installing boards until you reach the right edge (step 7). Use plenty of adhesive and drive several nails when you hit a wall stud. If none of the wall studs align beneath carsiding joints, tack the board that falls over a wall stud by face-nailing once at the top and once at the bottom. In most cases, you should be able to tack each board at the top too, nailing through the face and into the stud wall cap plate (this will be concealed by crown molding anyway). *Note: The mounting boards for the towel hooks will help hold the carsiding in place once they are attached at stud locations.*

Cut the towel hook backer boards to length from 1 × 6 stock. For a more decorative effect, cut a chamfer profile into the edges (or just the top and bottom edges) with a router and chamfering bit.

Install the backer board by driving 2½" deck screws, countersunk, at wall stud locations. Fill the screw holes with wood putty.

Install quarter-round molding around the bottom of the cabinet to conceal the gap where it meets the floor. Also install quarter-round to conceal the gap where the carsiding meets the cabinet seatboard (step 8). Make mitered returns at the end for a more finished appearance.

Attach crown molding to the top of the project (step 9), also making a mitered return to finish the ends of the molding.

Sand all wood surfaces and fill nail holes, screw holes, and visible gaps with wood putty. Paint the project with primer and at least two coats of enamel paint. Finally, attach the towel hooks to the towel hook backers.

Drive a pneumatic brad through the tongue of one of the far-right boards and into a marked wall stud.

Install quarter-round or base shoe molding at the top edge of the seatboard where it meets the carsiding. Tie the molding back to the wall with mitered returns.

Attach crown molding at the top of the project, creating mitered returns at the ends. Mark the ceiling joists with tape.

Glass Shelves

Glass shelving is unobtrusive so it can fit many styles of bathrooms—from sleek modern to elaborate Victorian. You can find a wide variety of shelving available in home stores and online.

Most glass shelves are held in place with metal mounts. How the shelves are secured to the mounts differs and how the mounts are attached to the wall also differs. Most shelves have a hidden bracket that is secured to the wall. The mount then slips over the bracket and is secured with a setscrew. The most basic models may have mounts that are screwed directly into the wall with exposed screws. The directions here are for shelving that uses hidden brackets.

If you are installing shelves on a tiled wall, mount the brackets in grout lines if at all possible to minimize the possibility of cracking the tiles. Many glass shelves have some flexibility in the distance between the mounts.

Tools & Materials ▸

Eye protection
Pencil
Level
Drill

Glass shelf with
    mounting
    hardware

Glass shelves fit any style and size of bathroom. They are held in place with metal mounts, which can be decorative, that are attached to the wall.

How to Install a Glass Shelf

Assemble the shelf and shelf holders (not the brackets). Hold the shelf against the wall in the desired location. On the wall, mark the center point of each holder, where the setscrew is.

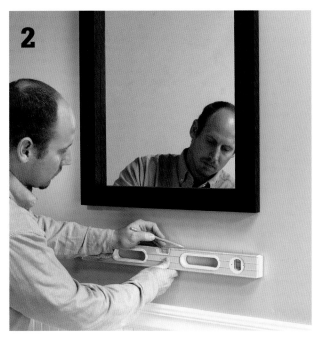

Remove the shelves and use the level to extend the mark into a 3" vertical line. Use the level to mark a horizontal line across the centers of these lines.

Center the middle round hole of the bracket over the intersection of the vertical and horizontal lines. Mark the center of each of the oblong holes. Put the bracket aside and drill a ¼" hole at each mark. Insert the included wall anchors in the holes. Replace the bracket and insert the screws into the wall anchors and drive the screws. Repeat for the second bracket.

Remove the shelf from the holders. Slide a holder over a bracket, check that the shelf mount is level, and tighten the setscrew. Repeat with the other holder. Insert the shelf and fix in place. Check the shelf for level. If it's not level, remove one holder and loosen the bracket screws. Slide the bracket up or down to make the unit level. Replace the holder and shelf.

Bedrooms & Closets

Bedrooms and closets are natural areas to tackle together, since order in the bedroom is so heavily dependent on adequate storage space in the closet. Of course, closets play a big role in many other areas, too. Each has its own role and challenges, but the primary storage goal remains the same: making the most of the available space while ensuring the most frequently used items are also the most easily accessible.

So how do you make a closet—a big box with a door—fit its contents? By outfitting it with modular storage components and accessories. These easy-to-install products go way beyond the simple shelf-and-rod setup that most closets are equipped with, and you can buy them as either complete integrated kits or a la carte add-ons. You might find that the range of products sold at your local home center or storage outlet store can be a little daunting. But once you pare down and prioritize your stuff for each closet, you'll be able to shop smart for the shelves and other fittings that will turn your catch-all closet spaces into dynamic, efficient storage systems.

In this chapter:

- Storage Strategies
- Closet System
- New Closet
- Closet Organizer
- Underbed Storage
- Chest of Drawers
- Armoire
- Headboard
- Shoe Cubby
- Tie & Belt Rack

Storage Strategies

As one of the few private places in a home, a bedroom is often expected to store more than just clothing. It may be the only room that's quiet enough for office work or peaceful enough for yoga. And many bedrooms are favorite retreats for reading and end up doubling as libraries. Your bedroom can be whatever it needs to be, but keep in mind that organizer pros recommend not losing sight of the bedroom's essential function as a place for rest. Crowding your sleeping area with activity-related stuff can be symbolic of how that activity takes priority over sleep and relaxation. In other words, a bedroom should look like a bedroom, not like a library with a bed.

A bedroom also should not become a last stop for items that haven't yet found a good home somewhere else. Perhaps you're storing important documents in your bedroom closet so they won't get mixed in with household paperwork. Or maybe you stash luggage under the bed, reasoning that the bedroom is where you do your packing. But really, shouldn't those papers be kept in a safe or a locked file drawer? And how often do you have to pack for a trip? If it's only a few times a year, maybe the luggage should go into the basement, attic, or garage to free up the underbed space for storing shoes and other everyday items.

The point is, the bedroom has enough legitimate storage needs without the extra burden of things that don't serve the room's daily routine. A good, honest decluttering of your bedroom will not only help you rid the room of excess baggage, it will help you think about your ideal uses of the space. Trimming the fat from your wardrobe is also the first step of a bedroom closet makeover. Here are some thoughts on popular storage options (some familiar, some new) for bedroom stuff:

Storage Furniture

A dresser, armoire, bureau, or chest of drawers is an obvious storage option in the bedroom. But if you're shopping for a new piece, be sure to consider the stuff you need to store in it. Drawers in a variety of sizes and depths are more efficient than uniformly large drawers. Alternatively, you can make big drawers more practical with organizer trays specifically designed to hold ties, hosiery, jewelry, or other small items.

For avid readers, a bookshelf adds the right touch to a bedroom setting. A low bookshelf can double as a nightstand or bedside table, while the top of a three- or four-shelf unit can be used like a dresser top and hold photos, lamps, or a tray for dropping pocket items at the end of the day.

Built-in furniture, such as this bed with drawers set into an attic, often makes the best use of odd bedroom spaces.

Nightstands & Bedside Tables

Bedside furniture can add both function and convenient storage to a bedroom. Units with drawers are good for hiding personal items and the jumble of bedtime necessities like reading glasses, ear plugs, medicines, etc. Open shelf space is ideal for bedtime bookworms. Always be sure the top of the piece offers enough room for a lamp, along with a book, water glass, alarm clock, and anything else you need to reach from bed.

Under the Bed

Here's a doozy of a storage space that's often overlooked. Underbed bins are great for stowing shoes, blankets, bedding, or out-of-season clothes (bins are essential for keeping stored items clean, orderly, and easily accessible). You can buy underbed containers in a range of styles and sizes, or you can build your own custom-sized boxes.

Headboard

A headboard can be much more than a decorative wood panel. Why not take advantage of this underutilized space for book and display shelving? Or perhaps integrate some wall-hung shelving or drawer units with a shelf spanning across the top of the headboard? A custom cabinetry unit, like the headboard project on page 114, can add loads of storage space combined with integrated nightstand pieces.

Bedside units with some concealed storage spaces and/or shelving are more functional and make better use of floor space than simple bedside tables.

Storing shoes in an underbed container takes a little more effort than grabbing them off of a shelf, but it sure frees up a lot of closet space. It's a good plan for all but your favorite everyday shoes.

Like the headboard space, the foot of the bed does a nice job accommodating added storage units. A blanket chest here can hold loads of bedding and provide bench seating for dressing.

Free up valuable closet space by utilizing the underbed area to store clothing. These built-in clothing storage compartments beautifully blend with the room's other decorative elements.

Walls

Although it's not commonly done, there's no reason a bedroom's walls can't be used for storage. With careful placement, you can make use of wall-hung cabinets, shelving units, or continuous shelving that runs around the perimeter of the room just below the ceiling. In a casual or rustic room setting, you can borrow from Shaker design and add a peg rail along one or more walls; clothing and other items can be hung on the pegs for storage and decoration.

Often the wall area above a bed can be dead-air space—perfect for creative custom units or for lofted beds.

Custom Closets

As lifestyles and purchasing habits have changed over the years, closet spaces appear to be getting smaller and smaller. But the truth is, most homes are built with inadequate closet space to begin with. Bedroom closets are particularly problematic: the standard-issue single hanger rod and shelf are OK for hanging some clothes and stacking sweaters and a few boxes above, but what about everything else—the shoes, hats, ties, belts, scarves, jewelry, purses? By taking inventory of your wardrobe (or other closet items in different rooms) and installing an organizer system, you can create a place for everything and have less trouble keeping everything in its place.

Basic closet system components generally come in two materials: wire and melamine-covered particleboard. For most reach-in closets, either type fits the bill, and you can always mix and match materials as needed. However, for shelves that will hold stacks of clothes (especially sweaters and fine knits), melamine parts are better because wire can leave an imprint on fabrics. If you prefer the look of real wood, you can build your own components with solid stock or nice veneer plywood, or shop around for higher-end prefab parts and systems.

Here's the basic planning process for outfitting a standard closet with modular components:

1. Go through the entire contents of the closet and weed out anything you no longer need or wear. Also pull out any pieces that can go into long-term seasonal storage.
2. Hang up all hanging items and group them by length: short-hang (shirts and blazers), medium-hang (unfolded pants, medium coats), and long-hang (long dresses and coats). Measure the length of hanger rod needed to accommodate each grouping. Also measure the longest item (from the rod down) in each group.
3. Arrange folded clothing in neat stacks, grouped by type. Measure the dimensions of each stack and grouping.
4. Decide which additional items should have a dedicated storage space or compartment, then measure and/or count the items.
5. Measure the dimensions of the closet space.
6. Think about your ideal closet arrangement, then start shopping (with your measurements in hand) to check out products and discuss your project with store staff. All that's left after that is the installation.

Accessories are made to fit with other parts in modular closet components. This glide-out tie/belt rack mounts right into the predrilled shelf pin holes of a vertical divider piece.

Variable hanger heights are key to space efficiency in a bedroom closet. Long-hang areas accommodate long skirts, shirts, or dresses. Short-hang areas can have two stacked rods (about 40" apart is standard) to double the hanging space.

Drawers are best for small items and are easy to integrate with shelves and other components. A multidrawer unit like this can be used in place of a conventional dresser to save on bedroom floor space.

A bank of adjustable shelves is ideal for assorted folded clothes. Try to keep shelf spaces short so the stacks are conveniently small. If your closet is deep enough, choose a deeper (16" or so) top shelf to provide better support for large bins and boxes. Add slanted shelves for convenient shoe storage as well.

Closet System

An adjustable closet system puts clothes and accessories within reach for people of all sizes. Build your own closet system to attain accessibility features like roll-under space, as well as adjustable shelves and rods. Add closet accessories, such as hooks, additional rods or shelves, pull-out drawers, baskets, slide-out belt and shoe racks, and fold-down pants racks to customize your system.

The closet organizer shown here can be adapted to fit almost any closet. It is a simple plywood cabinet with three adjustable shelves and space above and below for additional storage and easy access. Use finish-grade plywood for the cabinet and support piece. Then paint, stain, or protect the wood with a clear finish. Solid wood trim covers the plywood edges and lends strength to the shelves. For this, you can use clear pine or a hardwood such as poplar, oak, or maple. The shelves shown in this project are 11" deep. You may want to make them deeper. Just keep in mind that shelves longer than 36" may require additional support to prevent sagging.

This complete closet organizing system has a place for practically every stitch of your wardrobe.

Tools, Materials & Cutting List ▸

Tools

Work gloves
Eye protection
Tape measure
Circular saw
Straightedge cutting
  guide
Drill/driver

Router w/straight bit
Framing square
Stud finder
Level
Clamps
Hammer
Nail set

Key	Part	Dimension
A	(1) Cabinet back	$\frac{1}{2} \times 37\frac{1}{2} \times 77\frac{1}{4}$" plywood
B	(2) Cabinet sides	$\frac{1}{2} \times 11\frac{7}{8} \times 77\frac{1}{4}$" plywood
C	(1) Side support	$\frac{1}{2} \times 11\frac{7}{8} \times 77\frac{1}{4}$" plywood
D	(1) Cabinet top	$\frac{1}{2} \times 11\frac{7}{8} \times 36$" plywood
E	(1) Cabinet bottom	$\frac{1}{2} \times 11\frac{7}{8} \times 36$" plywood
F	(3) Shelves	$\frac{1}{2} \times 11\frac{7}{8} \times 35\frac{7}{8}$" plywood
G	(7) Trim	$1 \times 2^*$ pine

*Cut to fit

Materials

Pine or hardwood
  trim
  $(1 \times 1, 1 \times 2)$
Finish grade plywood
  $(\frac{1}{2}", \frac{3}{4}")$
2" coarse-thread
  drywall screws
4d finish nails
Wood glue
Wood finishing
  materials
$1\frac{1}{4}$"-dia. × 6 ft. closet
  rod

37½"   12½"

D

75"

Closet
rod

G

Standards

F

1x2 trim &
shelf edging

B

A

F

Closet
rod

G

G

G

F

G

G

E

77¼"

B

C

G

How to Build an Adjustable Closet Organizing System

Cut the plywood into narrow strips to create the cabinet sides and the shelves. A circular saw and a straightedge cutting guide work well for this task. If you have a table saw or a panel-cutting saw, you'll probably want to use one of those.

Cut grooves in the cabinet sides to accept the shelf standards. A router with a straight bit and cutting guide is a good tool choice here. Do not try to make the cuts in a single pass; use several passes of increasing depth.

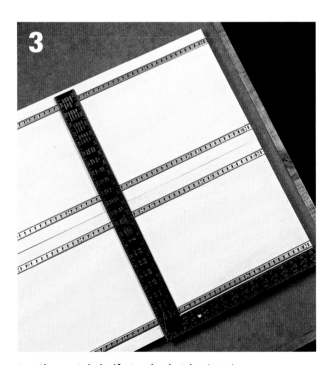

Lay the metal shelf standard strips into the grooves. Check with a square to make sure that the slots in the standards are aligned. If not, adjust one of the strips until they are, mark it, and then trim off the top. Install the standards.

Assemble the cabinet. Glue the cabinet top and bottom pieces between the ends of the cabinet sides. Make sure the outside faces of the top and bottom are flush with the ends of the sides. Before the glue dries, fasten the back panel to the cabinet using 2" coarse-thread drywall screws driven every 12".

5

Install the face frame. Cut trim pieces as well as the shelf edging. Attach the face frame members to the front edge of the cabinet with glue and 4d finish nails driven into pilot holes. Set the nail heads with a nail set.

6

Mount the cabinet to the back wall of the closet by driving screws through the back panel and into wall studs. Set the cabinet up on blocking to cerate storage space below. Make sure the cabinet is level before attaching it.

7

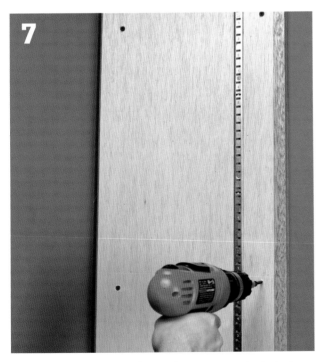

Install side supports and any other system parts, fastening into wall studs wherever possible. Add closet rods and other accessories.

Shelf supports ▸

Shelf support pegs, pins, and clips come in a very wide range of styles and sizes. Make sure the hardware you are planning to use is designed to work with the standards you've already installed. The spring clips seen here provide good holding power and are easy to remove and relocate.

New Closet

Closets are undoubtedly one of the most frequently used storage areas. Closets are used every day to store a wide variety of items from canned foods to sporting goods. Yet many people feel they have a lack of closet space because their existing closets are overflowing with items. If you have the space, building a new closet could be the solution to your storage problems.

The location and direction of the wall studs and ceiling joists are important to consider when planning the dimensions for your new closet. Whenever possible, position the walls of your closet so they can be anchored to ceiling joists and wall studs. Always maintain a minimum closet depth of 30".

Install all needed electrical and plumbing lines in the walls of the closet before hanging the wallboard. Make sure you comply with local building codes when building a closet. Many building codes require a permanent light fixture in closets.

The plan shown here presumes a room with 8-foot ceilings and a closet with a 32" door. If you alter the dimensions, then the sizes of the pieces will also change. Choose the style and size of the door for your closet before you begin the framing. The type of door you choose will determine the size of the rough opening needed for it.

After finishing the closet, install a closet rod or organizer to minimize wasted space. See page 100 for a good example of a closet organizer.

Install a built-in closet in a corner of any room to expand your storage space neatly and permanently. Use the double-plate design to install this closet anywhere, without having to install blocking above a finished ceiling.

Tools, Materials & Cutting List ▶

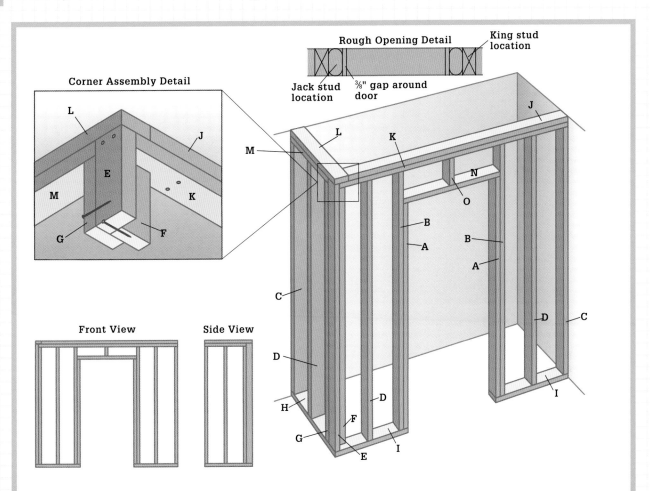

Rough Opening Detail

King stud location

Corner Assembly Detail

Jack stud location

⅜" gap around door

Front View   Side View

Tools

Work gloves
Eye protection
Stud finder
Framing square
Nail set
Circular saw
Drill/driver
Plumb bob
Chalk line
Hammer
Wallboard knives
Wallboard lifter
Level
Tape measure
Ladder
Sand paper

Materials

Corner bead
Door casings
2 × 4" × 8 ft. pine studs (17)
Common nails (10d, 16d)
8d casing nails
1¼" wallboard screws
Wallboard tape
Wallboard compound
½" × 4 × 8 ft. wallboard (6)
32 × 80" prehung interior door kit
Shims
Finishing materials

Key	Part	Dimension
A	(2) Jack stud	1½ × 3½ × 83½"
B	(2) King stud	1½ × 3½ × 91½"
C	(2) End stud	1½ × 3½ × 91½"
D	(3) Intermediate stud	1½ × 3½ × 91½"
E	(1) Outside corner stud	1½ × 3½ × 93"
F	(1) Inside corner stud	1½ × 3½ × 91½"
G	(1) Corner stud	1½ × 3½ × 91½"
H	(1) Side wall sole plate	1½ × 3½ × 31½"
I	(2) Front wall sole plate	1½ × 3½ × 30"
J	(1) Upper top plate, front wall	1½ × 3½ × 90½"
K	(1) Lower top plate, front wall	1½ × 3½ × 92½"
L	(1) Upper top plate, side wall	1½ × 3½ × 35"
M	(1) Lower top plate, side wall	1½ × 3½ × 31½"
N	(1) Cripple stud	1½ × 3½ × 6½"
O	(1) Header	1½ × 3½ × 37"

How to Add a Closet

1

2

3

Examine your walls and ceiling to locate framing members and internal wall components such as wiring and ductwork so you can select a closet location and size that make sense. Start the construction process by attaching a cap plate for the main closet wall to the ceiling joists.

Add sole plates for the closet wall. The plates should be directly below the cap plates. Use a plumb bob to transfer the location downward.

Install a second cap plate, and then attach wall studs so they run from the sole plate to the cap plate and are plumb. Drive 8d nails toenail-style to attach studs to the cap plate.

4

5

6

Toenail the corner stud assembly in place with 10d nails. Follow the Corner Detail drawing on page 97 for the exact placement of the studs.

Endnail the door header flush with the reference marks indicating the height of the jack studs.

Drive 10d nails through the top of the header into the top ends of the jack studs. Also nail the jack studs to the king studs.

7

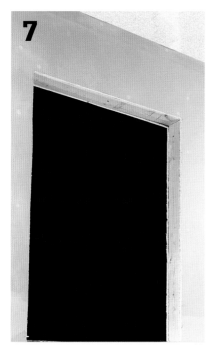

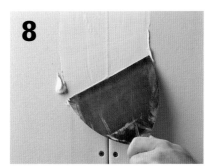

8

9

Cover the stud wall with drywall. Plan the drywall placement so there are no joints at the corners of the door opening. You can finish just the exterior side, or you can drywall the interior of the closet as well.

Tape seams and cover with joint compound. First, lay a bed of joint compound at each seam (upper) and then press drywall tape into the seam. Add more joint compound over the tape, feathering it out.

Install metal corner bead around all exposed outside corners, taking care not to overdrive fasteners and crimp the bead. Cover the bead with joint compound.

10

11

Option: Finish the interior closet walls with drywall, paneling or tongue-and-groove aromatic cedar.

Hang the closet door. For convenience, use a prehung interior passage door. Paint the closet walls.

Install the door casings using 8d finish nails driven through pilot holes and into the wall framing.

Closet Organizer

One of the best ways to maximize the capacity of your closet is to install an organizer that is tailored to your specific storage needs. This closet organizer was designed with a bedroom closet in mind, but it could be adapted for a pantry or entryway closet. With a custom-built central shelf unit, items such as shoes, blankets, and sweaters stay organized. The two upper shelves are perfect for accessory items or seasonal clothing. Best of all, you can build this organizer for a five-foot closet for the cost of a single sheet of plywood, a clothes rod, and a few feet of 1 × 3 lumber.

Make efficient use of your closet space with an easy-to-build closet organizer.

Tools, Materials & Cutting List ▸

Tools

Work gloves
Eye protection
Hammer
Tape measure

Framing square
Circular saw
Screwdriver
Level

Materials

Finish nails (6d, 8d)
¾" × 4 × 8 ft. finish-grade plywood
1 × 3 pine lumber
1¼"-dia. × 6 ft. clothes rod
Clothes-rod brackets
Wood glue
Finish materials

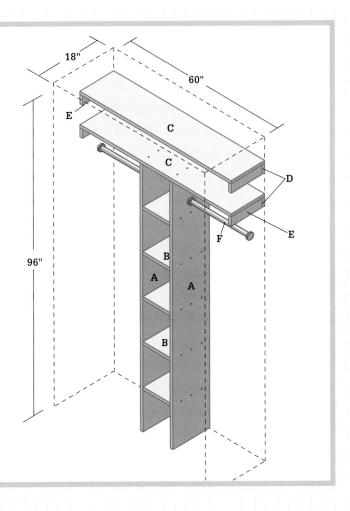

Key	Part	Dimension
A	(2) Central shelf side	¾ × 11⅞ × 76" plywood
B	(5) Shelf	¾ x11⅞ × 11⅞" plywood
C	(2) Upper shelf	¾ × 11⅞" × 5 ft. plywood
D	(2) Back wall support	¾ × 2½" × 5 ft. pine
E	(4) End wall support	¾ × 2½ × 20" pine
F	(2) Clothes pole	1¼"-dia. × 6 ft. closet pole

How to Build a Closet Organizer

1

Install shelf cleats in the closet to support the upper and lower shelves. Use 1 × 3 or 1 × 4, making sure to drive fasteners at stud locations.

2

Assemble the central shelving unit by nailing or screwing the plywood components together. Reinforce the joints with glue. Leave the top of the unit open.

3

Attach the lower shelf to the central unit and the wall cleats, and attach the upper shelf to all three wall cleats. Paint or stain the organizer as desired.

Underbed Storage

A standard twin-size bed conceals at least 15 cubic feet of storage space beneath the box spring. Put that valuable space to good use with this underbed storage box. Designed to roll easily in and out from under your bed, it is the perfect spot to store just about anything. And if you use aromatic cedar for the compartment lids, clothing items will be safe from moths and other pests.

Construction of the underbed storage box is very simple. It is basically a pine frame with a center divider and cleats for the lids and the bottom panels. We mounted bed-box rollers at all four corners so the box can slide easily. Bed-box rollers are special wheels that can be purchased at most hardware stores or woodworker's stores—because they are hard plastic, they will not damage or discolor your carpeting.

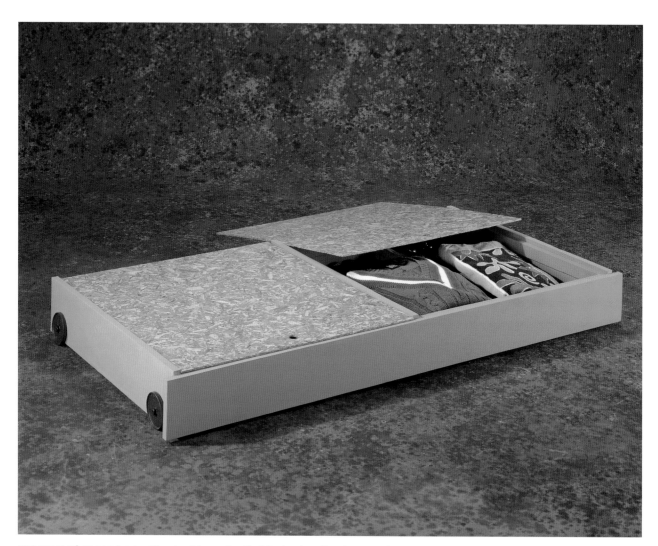

Put wasted space beneath a bed to work with this simple roll-out storage box.

Tools, Materials & Cutting List ▶

Tools
Work gloves
Eye protection
Circular saw
Jigsaw
Pipe clamps
Drill with 1" bit
Screwdriver
Power sander
Tape measure
Hand sander

Materials
Pine lumber (1 × 2, 1 × 3, 1 × 6)
Plywood (½", ⅜")
¼" × 4 × 8 ft. aromatic cedar
Bed-box rollers
Wood screws (#6 × 1⅜", 2")
Wood glue
Sand paper
Wood putty
Finishing materials

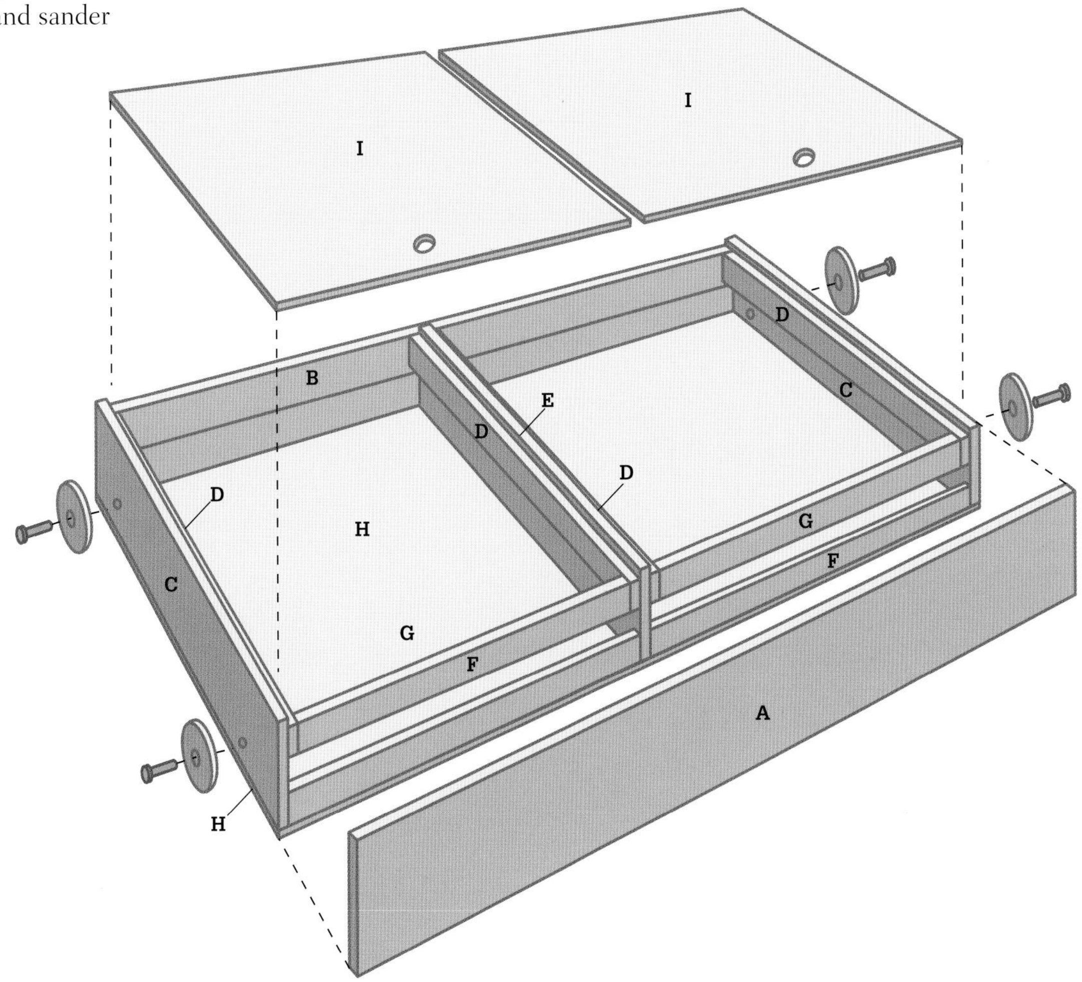

Key	Part	Dimension
A	(1) Box front	¾ × 5½" × 5 ft. pine
B	(2) Box back	¾ × 2½ × 56½" pine
C	(2) Box side	¾ × 5½ × 29¼" pine
D	(4) Lid support	¾ × 1½ × 28½" pine

Key	Part	Dimension
E	(1) Divider	¾ × 5½ × 28½" pine
F	(2) Bottom cleat	¾ × 1½ × 27¾" pine
G	(2) Top cleat	¾ × 1½ × 26¼" pine
H	(1) Bottom panel	⅜ × 29½ × 58" plywood
I	(2) Sliding lid	¼ × 27¾ × 29¼" aromatic cedar

How to Build an Under-bed Storage Box

STEP A: MAKE THE FRAME.
The frame for the under-bed storage box is a basic box made with butt joints. The front board on the box overhangs the sides by 1" to conceal the front bed-box rollers that are mounted to the sides.

1. Cut the box front (A) and box sides (C) to length from 1 × 6 pine, and cut the box backs (B) from 1 × 3 pine. When laid edge to edge, two 1 × 3s are ½" shorter than one 1 × 6, which will create a recess for mounting the bottom panel. Sand all parts smooth.
2. Draw a reference line on the inside face of the box front 1" in from each side. Set the box front on a spacer made from ½" plywood. Align the box sides at the inside edges of the reference lines (make sure the box front is ⁵⁄₁₆" higher than the top of the sides).
3. Attach the sides to the front using glue and #6 × 2" wood screws. Counterbore the screws so the heads can be covered with wood putty. Attach one of the box back 1 × 3s between the sides, flush with the bottom edges using glue and screws.
4. Attach the other 1 × 3 between the sides, making sure the edges of the two back parts are butted together tightly and that there is a ½" gap between the top of the back and the sides.

STEP B: INSTALL THE FRAME DIVIDER & CLEATS.

1. Mark the centerpoints on the inside faces of the box front and box backs. The front centerpoint is 30" from each end. The back centerpoint is 28¼" from each end (measure from the ends of the back, not the outside faces of the box).
2. Cut the divider (E), then position it between the front and the back of the box, with the end of the divider centered on the centerpoints. The top of the divider should be ⁵⁄₁₆" above the top edges of the front and back.
3. Attach the divider with glue and screws driven through the front and back, into the ends of the divider. Cut the lid supports (D), top cleats (G), and bottom cleats (F).
4. Attach the lid supports to the sides of the divider, flush with the tops of the front and back. Use glue and #6 × 1¾" wood screws.

STEP C: ATTACH THE CLEATS.

1. Attach the bottom cleats to the inside face of the box front, flush with the bottom edges of the sides.

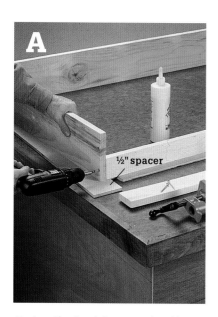

Fasten the back between the sides with wood glue and counterbored screws. Keep the bottom flush with spacers.

Clamp the lid supports in position flush with the top of the box in front and back, then fasten them with wood glue and screws.

Attach the cleats to the inside face of the box front, trimming them if necessary. Cut the bottom panel to size.

2. Position the top cleats between the lid supports against the inside face of the box front. If the cleats are too long, mark and trim them to length. Attach the top cleats to the inside face of the box front flush with the tops of the lid supports.

STEP D: ATTACH THE BOTTOM PANEL.

1. Cut the bottom panel (H) to size from ⅜" plywood. Turn the frame assembly upside down and apply glue to the bottom edges of the frame components. Fasten the bottom panel into the frame assembly by driving screws through the bottom into the edges of the frame and the divider.

STEP E: INSTALL THE LIDS & APPLY FINISHING TOUCHES.

1. Cut the sliding lids (I) to size from ¼"-thick aromatic cedar pressboard. Mark centerpoints (13⅞" from the sides) 2" in from the front edge of each lid.

2. Drill 1"-dia. holes through the centerpoints to create finger grips for sliding the lids back and forth. Sand the edges of the lids as well as the finger-grip cutouts to prevent splinters when handling the lids. The lids are designed to simply rest on the lid supports. Because they are not attached permanently, they can be lifted off for easy access or slid back and forth.

3. Fill all counterbored screw holes with wood putty, then sand the entire unit with fine or medium sandpaper.

4. Install the bed-box rollers on the outside faces of the sides, 3" in from the front and back. The rollers should extend ½" below the bottom edges of the sides. Remove the rollers and axles before finishing. We painted the storage box, then added a coat of polyurethane (except for the cedar lids, which were left unfinished to maintain their fragrance).

5. Reinstall the rollers after the finish dries. You may choose to mount chest handles or straps (optional) on the front to make it easier to slide the box in and out from under the bed.

Fasten the bottom panel to the box frame and divider.

Mount bed-box rollers on the outside faces of the sides so the rollers extend ½" below the box bottom.

Chest of Drawers

Children's furniture is notoriously expensive, but you can build this simple chest of drawers for a fraction of the cost of a dresser from most specialty shops. To make it, you'll use only the most basic carpentry techniques to achieve a result with a clean, attractive appearance.

This chest of drawers features all wood parts—there is no need to purchase metal drawer slides or other hardware. Not quite full-size, this chest of drawers will fit nicely into your child's bedroom, while still offering plenty of clothing storage space. It also makes a great nightstand.

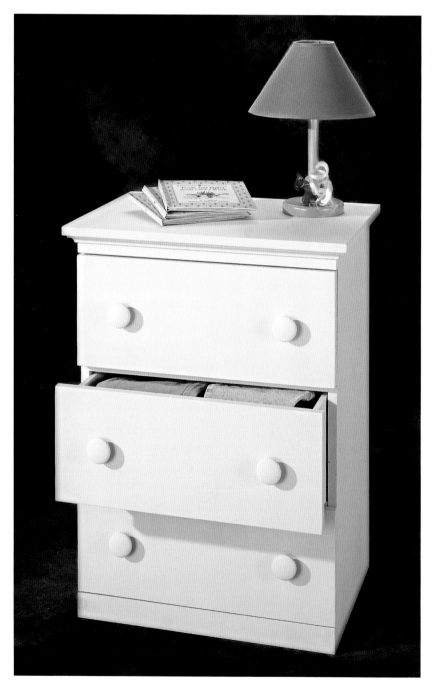

This petite chest of drawers brings clothing into reach for young children, yet provides generous storage space for an older child's outfits.

Tools, Materials & Cutting List ▸

Tools

Work gloves
Eye protection
Circular saw
Drill with bits
Finish sander
Sand paper

Hammer
Router
Miter box
Tape measure

Plywood (¼", ½", ¾")
1 × 2 pine lumber
Straightedge
½" quarter-round
  molding

Materials

Tape
¾" cove molding
Wood glue
Wood screws
  (#6 × 1¼", 2")
4d finish nails
1" brad nails
Plastic drawer
  glides (24)
2"-dia. cabinet
  drawer knobs
  (6)
Wood putty
Finishing
  materials

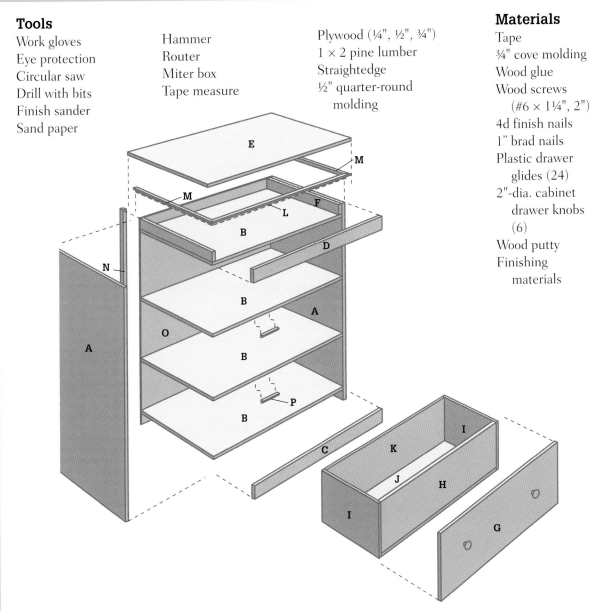

Key	Part	Dimension
A	(2) Side	¾ × 15¼ × 31" plywood
B	(4) Duster	¾ × 14½ × 20½" plywood
C	(1) Bottom rail	¾ × 2 × 22" plywood
D	(1) Top rail	¾ × 1½ × 22" plywood
E	(1) Top	¾ × 17" × 2 ft. plywood
F	(2) Top cleat	¾ × 1½ × 14½" pine
G	(3) Drawer face	¾ × 9 × 22" plywood
H	(3) Drawer front	¾ × 7¼ × 19¼" plywood

Key	Part	Dimension
I	(6) Drawer side	½ × 8 × 14¼" plywood
J	(3) Drawer bottom	¾ × 13¾ × 19¼" plywood
K	(3) Drawer back	½ × 8 × 19¼" plywood
L	(1) Front cove	¾ × ¾ × 23½" molding
M	(2) Side cove	¾ × ¾ × 16¾" molding
N	(2) Back cleat	½ × ½ × 29⅜" molding
O	(1) Back	¼ × 20½ × 29⅜" plywood
P	(3) Stop block	½ × ½ × 4" molding

How to Build a Chest of Drawers

Build the chest. Cut the sides, duster panels, and back panel to size. Mark guidelines for the duster positions on the inside faces of the sides, 1⅝", 10¾", 19⅞", and 29" from the bottoms. Stand the side pieces on their back edges and set ¾" spacers between them. Position the duster panels so their lower edges are flush with the marked guidelines and their front edges are flush with the front edges of the side panels. Fasten the duster panels in place using glue and 2" wood screws driven into countersunk pilot holes.

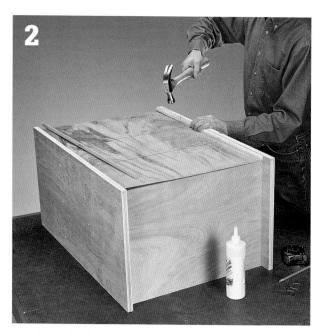

Install the back. Lay the back in place so its top edge is flush with the top edges of the sides. Fasten it with 1" brads driven through the back and into the duster panels. Cut the back cleats to size from ½" quarter-round molding, then attach these cleats to the back edges of the sides using 1" brads. Install the front rails and cabinet top.

Tack plastic drawer glides to the inside surfaces of the drawer opening to eliminate friction when the drawers slide.

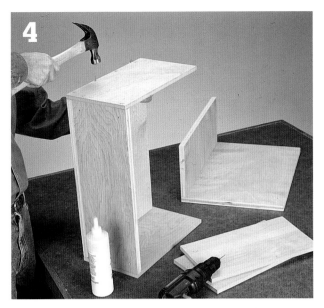

Build the drawer boxes. Cut the drawer fronts, drawer bottoms, drawer sides, and drawer backs to size. Fasten each drawer bottom to a drawer front with glue and counterbored 1¼" wood screws. Fasten the sides to the front and bottom with glue and 1" brads driven through the sides. Fasten the drawer backs to the back edges of the drawer sides and bottom using glue and 1" brads.

Attach drawer faces and hardware. Cut the drawer faces and round over all the edges. Tape a ¼"-thick spacer to the back of each drawer, and slide the drawers into the openings in the chest. The glides keep drawers centered and the spacers keep the front edges aligned. Attach the drawer faces, taping each face in place on the drawer front and then screwing it on with 1¼" screws driven from the inside of the drawer box. Maintain ⅛"-wide gaps between drawer faces. Attach knobs to the drawer faces. Most drawer knobs have a bolt in the center that is inserted through the drawer front to secure the knob.

Apply the finishing touches. Miter cut the front cove and side cove with matching 45° angles, and install them into the frame where the top is joined to the chest using 4d finish nails. Cut the stop blocks to size. Remove the drawers and fasten the blocks on the duster panel bottoms ¾" from their front edges using 1" brads. Fill all nail and screw holes and exposed plywood edges with wood putty, then sand all the surfaces smooth. Prime and paint the dresser as desired.

Armoire

Long before massive walk-in closets became the norm in residential building design, homeowners and apartment dwellers compensated for cramped bedroom closets by making or buying armoires. The trim armoire design shown here reflects the basic styling developed during the heyday of the armoire, but at a scale that makes it usable in just about any living situation. At 60" high and only 36" wide, this compact armoire still boasts plenty of interior space. Five shelves on the left side are sized to store folded sweaters and shirts. You can hang several suit jackets or dresses in the closet section to the right.

With a simple, rustic appearance, this moveable closet blends into almost any bedroom.

Tools, Materials & Cutting List ▸

Tools

Work gloves
Eye protection
Circular saw
Drill with bits
Jigsaw
Finish sander

Sanding block
Framing square
Bar or pipe clamps
Hammer

Utility knife
Household iron
Veneer edge tape
Compass

Materials

Birch Plywood (½", ¾")
Pine lumber (1 × 2,
   1 × 3, 1 × 6)
1½"-dia. × 2 ft. fir dowel
Wood screws (#6 × 1¼")
Finish nails (3d, 6d)
Wood glue
Nail set
Closet rod hangers
Hinges (6)
Door pulls (3)
Finishing materials

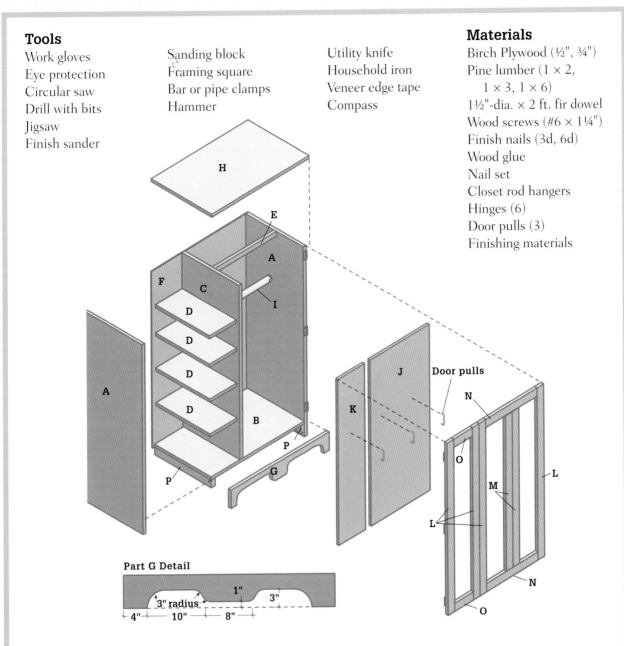

Part G Detail

3" radius
1"
3"
4"   10"   8"

Key	Part	Dimension
A	(2) Side panel	¾ × 21 × 59¼" plywood
B	(1) Bottom panel	¾ × 21 × 34½" plywood
C	(1) Center panel	¾ × 21 × 53¾" plywood
D	(4) Shelf	¾ × 10⅞ × 20¼" plywood
E	(1) Stringer	¾" × 1½ × 22⅞" pine
F	(1) Back	¼" × 36 × 54½" plywood
G	(1) Front skirt	¾" × 5½" × 3 ft. pine
H	(1) Top panel	¾ × 22" × 3 ft. plywood

Key	Part	Dimension
I	(1) Closet rod	1½"-dia. × 22⅞" fir dowel
J	(1) Closet door panel	¾ × 22⁷⁄₁₆ × 52⅛" plywood
K	(1) Shelf door panel	¾ × 10⁷⁄₁₆ × 52⅛" plywood
L	(4) Door stile	¾ × 2½ × 53⅝" pine
M	(2) False stile	¾ × 2½ × 48⅝" pine
N	(2) Closet door rail	¾ × 2½ × 18¹⁵⁄₁₆" pine
O	(2) Shelf door rail	¾ × 2½ × 6¹⁵⁄₁₆" pine
P	(2) Cleat	¾ × 1½ × 21" pine

How to Build an Armoire

1

2

Apply veneer edge tape to the exposed plywood edges. Trim off excess tape with a sharp utility knife.

Clamp the bottom panel between the sides and fasten it to the cleats using glue and finish nails. Install center panel using glue and finish nails.

3

4

Fasten the shelves between the side panel and center panel with glue and 6d finish nails.

Nail the ¼"-thick back panel to the back edges of the carcass to help keep it square.

5

Use a compass to mark the decorative cutout at the bottom of the front skirt board. Then cut the curves using a jigsaw.

6

Fasten the top panel with glue and 6d finish nails.

7

Attach the rails and stiles to the door panels with glue. Drive 3d finish nails through the frames into the panels.

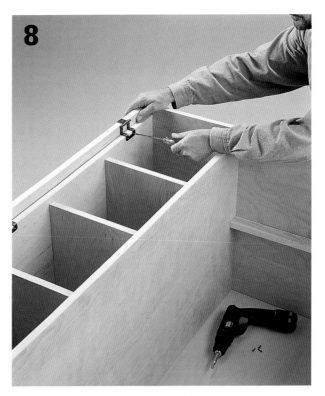

8

Position the doors and fasten the hinges to the side panels.

Headboard

An attached headboard isn't the only way to adorn the head of a bead. Indeed, it can be dressed not only with form but with terrific function. Combining cabinets of differing sizes and shapes provides a finished appearance to a bed in much the same way as an attractive but purely decorative headboard, but the cabinets also provide the utility of much needed storage with a built-in feel.

The clean, defined lines of the cabinets lend this bed surround a modern feel while the option for above-bed lighting creates the halo of a warm and calm space for starting and ending the day or tucking away for a quick nap.

Before getting started, determine if you want the option of cabinet-mounted lights. If so, rough-in the wires and switch(es) prior to installing the cabinets. Once the cabinets are on site, prep them before hanging by drilling the appropriate holes to accommodate the wires and house the light fixtures.

Assembled from stock cabinets, this surround defines sleeping space—useful in open-concept spaces or lofts—and provides storage.

Tools, Materials & Cutting List ▸

Tools

Work gloves
Eye protection
Tape measure
Pencil

Level ledger board
Drill/driver
Plumb bob

Combination square
Pull saw
Drywall patch
Caulk
Sandpaper

Materials

1 × 3 board
Filler strips (if
    necessary)
Clamps
Countertop material
Light fixtures and
    switches (optional)
Drywall screws
Shims
Cabinets

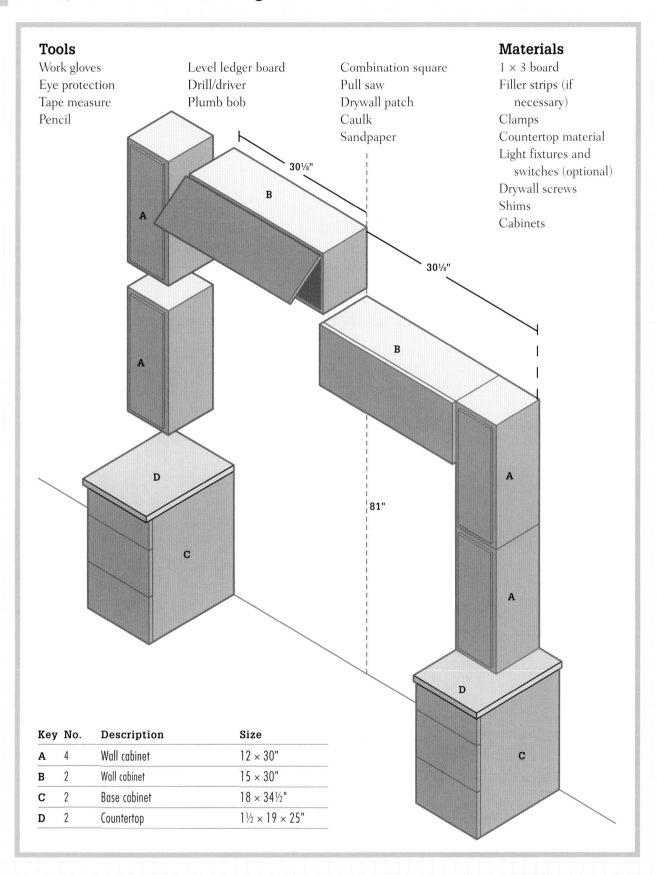

Key	No.	Description	Size
A	4	Wall cabinet	12 × 30"
B	2	Wall cabinet	15 × 30"
C	2	Base cabinet	18 × 34½"
D	2	Countertop	1½ × 19 × 25"

How to Build a Stock Cabinet Headboard

Begin installing the horizontal upper units. Before installation, mark the left and right edges of the project area and then mark a centerline between the edges. Temporarily attach a level ledger board to the wall just underneath the location for the cabinet bottoms. Install the horizontal uppers by resting them in position on the temporary ledgers and then driving drywall screws through the cabinet backs and into wall studs.

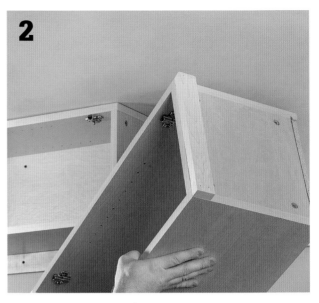

Install the next horizontal cabinet. In some cases you may find that there is a gap between adjoining cabinets. For example, in the installation seen here the two horizontal cabinets did not quite have enough combined length to span the distance necessary to accommodate the bed below. So a 1 × 2 filler strip was attached to the end of each cabinet where it meets the vertical cabinets. In conjunction with a filler strip added to the top inside edge of the vertical cabinet, this filled the gap. Install all upper units.

With the uppers installed, you now have rock solid control points to plumb down to the floor so you can place the lower cabinets accurately. Measure the base cabinet widths to the left and right of the plumb lines and mark the baseboard for removal. Using a combination square and pull saw, mark and remove the base molding. Be careful not to damage the wallboard when removing the base molding.

Begin installing the vertical cabinets, working from the top down. Drive shims behind the cabinets as needed to make sure the front edges of the face frames are in alignment.

5

Attach the horizontal cabinets to the top vertical cabinets by driving screws through the cabinet walls or through the face frames if your cabinets have them. If you have installed filler strips, make sure to attach to them from both sides.

6

Make and install a countertop on each base unit prior to installation. The base cabinets will need some type of countertop surface so they can function as nightstands and also support the vertical upper cabinets. We made particleboard countertops with plastic laminate applied to the tops and edges. Because the sizes are relatively small, this project also presents a good opportunity to experiment with some high-end countertop materials, such as granite or quartz.

7

Install the base cabinets in the project area, tight to the plumb lines. First, set the base cabinets into place and then set the lower vertical cabinets on top. Shim underneath the base cabinet (or build a small platform for larger gaps) to raise the base so the vertical cabinets form a clean joint. Remove the lower vertical cabinets and then attach the base cabinets by driving drywall screws through the cabinet backs and/or nailer strips and into wall studs.

8

Set the lower vertical cabinets back into place, shimming as necessary, and then fasten them to the wall studs with drywall screws. Install (or have installed) the light fixtures and switches. Remove the temporary ledger, patch drywall, caulk, and trim cabinet bases as required. Sand and spot-touch the finishes.

Shoe Cubby

This shoe cubby is designed to slide on top of a shelf in an existing unit. The vertical spacers are fixed to the top shelf, and all other shelving is adjustable. To ensure your cubby sides align with the verticals in the section the cubby will reside, it's crucial to have the entire custom closet unit level and plumb before attempting to cut cubby sides. This project is built using predrilled closet shelf standards and other professional-level closet system parts. You can find them for sale in closet specialty shops or you can make your own comparable parts using melamine-coated particleboard.

A shoe cubby with adjustable shelves, whether part of a larger closet system or a stand-alone item, offers an attractive and efficient way to organize your shoes and protect your footwear investment.

Tools, Materials & Cutting List ▸

Tools

Work gloves
Eye protection
Tape measure
Circular saw with
  melamine blade
Framing square
Drill with 20 mm
  bits
Rubber mallet

Materials

2½" drywall screws
Caps for screw
  holes
Screwdriver
Shelf pins (36)
Melamine-coated
  particle board

Key	Part	Dimension	Pcs.	Material
A	Cubby pars	24 × 12 × 18 ½"	2	¾" melamine shelf stock with predrilled pin holes
B	Fixed shelf	24 × 12"	1	¾" melamine shelf stock with predrilled pin holes
C	Adjustable shelves	7¾ × 12"	9	½" melamine

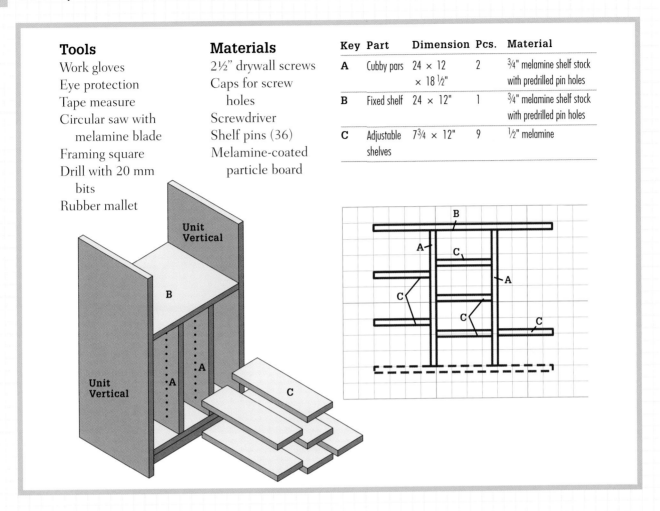

How to Build a Shoe Cubby

1

Measure from the floor or the base on which the cubby will sit up to the first of the predrilled shelf pinholes. Note this measure and cut all other vertical parts (if using predrilled stock) so the first hole is the same distance from the bottom edge.

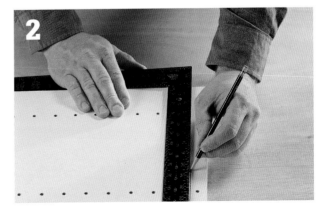

2

Transfer the measurement taken in step 1 to the other vertical parts and draw a cutting line at the same point using a square as a guide.

(continued)

Cut the vertical parts' top length along the cutting lines. Also cut the shelves and the top to length using either predrilled stock or a comparable undrilled material.

Fasten the fixed shelf to the vertical supports with coarse drywall screws driven into countersunk pilot holes. Use at least three 2½" screws per joint.

Mark and cut intermediate shelves to length so they will fit between the uprights, allowing a slight gap on each edge for shelf pins. Use a square to draw cutting lines.

Install the shelves. It is easiest to install adjustable shelving by first tilting it at a 45° angle, sliding it into place, and then lowering it down level onto the shelf pegs. Tap into place, if necessary.

Tie & Belt Rack

There are several tie and belt racks for sale. The manufacturer versions are often made to attach directly into the shelf pin holes on the verticals in your custom closet, making placement and adjustability a breeze. You can find those racks at home centers and online (see Resources on page 234). To make a custom tie and belt rack, follow the instructions given here. This heavy-duty cedar hanger will protect your winter coats from moth damage when used as a standard hanger, or it can keep your ties and belts organized and easily accessible.

Made of aromatic red cedar, the tie and belt rack organizes your accessories.

Tools, Materials & Cutting List ▶

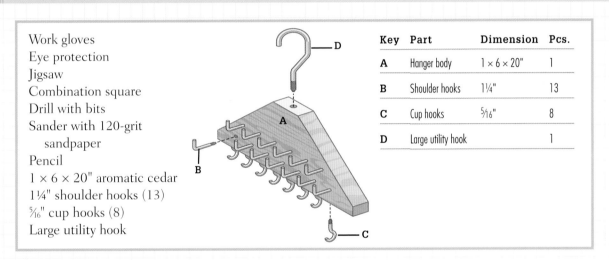

Work gloves
Eye protection
Jigsaw
Combination square
Drill with bits
Sander with 120-grit
   sandpaper
Pencil
1 × 6 × 20" aromatic cedar
1¼" shoulder hooks (13)
⁵⁄₁₆" cup hooks (8)
Large utility hook

Key	Part	Dimension	Pcs.
A	Hanger body	1 × 6 × 20"	1
B	Shoulder hooks	1¼"	13
C	Cup hooks	⁵⁄₁₆"	8
D	Large utility hook		1

How to Build a Tie & Belt Rack

1

Cut the aromatic cedar workpiece to size and shape using a jigsaw, applying even pressure—don't lean too hard into the cut.

2

Use a combination square to lay out reference marks for drilling guide holes for the cup hooks in the bottom edge of the rack.

3

Draw two rows of reference marks for the shoulder hooks, offsetting the rows by ¾" so they don't obstruct one another.

Living Areas

Because the common living areas are the most public rooms in the house, it is especially important that storage strategies here strike a balance between convenience and appearance. Convenience comes from having your things close to where you use them. Appearance is subject to your taste, of course, but also to your priorities: do you prefer the rooms to be clutter-free at all times, or are you comfortable with a more lived-in look? In general, can you put things away easily when it's time to clean up?

Another balancing act required for most living areas is the allocation of space for accommodating storage items vs. display items. Some useful things, such as books, lend themselves to both storage and display because they look good enough to be kept out in the open. Other stuff is best stored behind closed doors.

Finally, organizing your living spaces wouldn't be complete without some attention paid to entryways and connecting spaces. A good plan in high-traffic areas creates a welcome greeting to visitors, making them feel at home the moment they walk through the door.

In this chapter:

- Storage Strategies
- Storage Cubes
- Suspended Shelving
- Mudroom Wall System
- Understairs Bookcases
- Closet Office
- Kids' Stackable Storage Blocks
- Crown Molding Shelves
- Stock-Cabinet Hobby Center

Storage Strategies

Living room, family room, TV room, rumpus room—whatever you call your favorite hangouts, the storage strategy is pretty straightforward: satisfy every activity that takes place there while keeping clutter to a minimum. In most homes, this is accomplished with thoughtful room arrangement and careful selection and use of furniture and shelving.

Living Rooms & Family Rooms

In homes with more than one main living space, the living room tends to be centered around social gatherings and quiet family leisure activities. The furniture and layout are geared toward conversation, reading, or relaxing in front of the fireplace. Likewise, storage and display in the living room should reflect these themes of social interaction and hospitality while keeping personal items out of sight.

By contrast, the family room, or TV room, is often dominated by the television and media entertainment. It's also the usual place for kids' play areas and adjunct work zones such as a hobby table or home office tucked into a corner. Convenience and function are the reigning themes here, and it's often best to set up distinct activity zones so everyone can do their own thing at the same time.

If your home has only one main living space to support all of its leisure activities, a zoned arrangement can be most effective, as well as storage pieces that are adaptable for both casual family time and entertaining with guests.

The secret to accommodating storage needs in any living space is to substitute conventional furniture and accessories with pieces that do double duty: instead of a traditional sofa table behind the couch, use a long console unit with attractive doors and/or open shelving. Replace end tables and accent tables with credenzas. Prevent coffee table clutter by swapping your four-legged model with a boxy unit with integrated storage spaces. Even an ottoman can lend a hand if it has a lid and a hidden storage compartment inside.

A media center with plenty of enclosed storage space is a great way to keep the family room organized

Utilize flea market finds such as these antique filing units stacked atop one another, for a one-of-a-kind storage-oriented decor in living rooms.

Traditionally a dining room fixture, a sideboard (or buffet) is great for transitional areas, too. Here, a contemporary sideboard provides concealed storage for both the open dining area and adjacent living room.

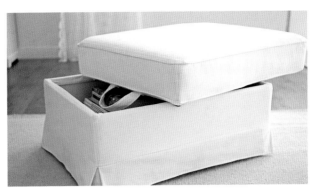

A full-service ottoman. This clever piece works as a footrest, a casual seat, a drink table, and a storage unit.

Shelving & Bookcase Basics

Shelves and bookcases are the storage workhorses of most living areas, filling odd spaces, defining zones in open-plan rooms, adding color and warmth to empty wall surfaces, and more. Here are some tips for making them work for your storage strategy:

- Use bookcases or banks of shelving as architectural details. For example, two cases meeting at an inside corner create a cozy reading nook; matching cases flanking a couch, sitting area, or bank of windows provide visual balance and help define the intermediate space; a continuous perimeter shelf running close to the ceiling adds a decorative effect similar to a cornice.

- Build custom shelves to fill nooks and oddly shaped walls.
- Arrange books for visual appeal (not just straight-up by size); lay some flat or at an angle; leave a little breathing room by not overcrowding the shelves; intersperse display items if desired.
- Conceal paperwork, old magazines, and other less-decorative material inside attractive file boxes or bins; use matching containers to prevent a cluttered look.
- Include some room for expanding your collection when buying or building new shelving.

There's more than one way to fill a bookcase. These pieces are also a great place to display photos, collectibles, or other decorative objects.

Shelves can fit just about anywhere. These store-bought bracketless shelves were laid out to follow the slope of the staircase. The longer shelves are made with multiple pieces butted together.

TV & Media Storage

Since flat-panel models became the standard, TVs aren't the decorator's nightmare they once were; the slim new sets are much easier to hide or to integrate with a room's décor than their bulky predecessors. At the same time, most people's tastes have changed, and showing off your hi-fi equipment isn't as cool as it was a few decades ago. So storing electronics can be a tricky one, especially when you're also dealing with multichannel sound systems and gaming equipment. The other problem is finding easy-access storage for hundreds of CDs and DVDs (and LPs, if you're still a hi-fi maven).

One elegant solution is to load everything into an all-in-one media console, the contemporary version of an entertainment center. Many consoles have divided-lite glass doors to put a decorative face over all those black boxes. Units with ample drawer space are best for storing CD and DVD cases. Another option is to mount the TV (assuming it's flat-panel) on the wall above a media console or sideboard that looks like a conventional furniture piece but has plenty of shelves for electronics. Units with solid doors keep the equipment out of view when you're not using it. You can fill the top of the console with books or decorative pieces to help blend the TV into the composition.

If you're looking for a home for an older tube TV, there are media stand units available with large top surfaces and storage shelving in a cabinet space below. However, before you spend a lot on a new specialty furniture unit, you should consider upgrading to a flat-panel TV, which gives you many more options for attractive storage. Keep in mind that electronics become obsolete (or simply stop working) in a matter of years, while a nice piece of furniture can last forever.

Dozens of disc cases stored out in the open can make a living room look like a college dorm. Instead, file your media in drawers fitted with plastic inserts or in pull-out organizers that fit on shelves and hide away behind a cabinet door.

TV and media storage can be both practical and (dare we say?) beautiful. This media console houses a full set of electronics, plus music and video discs. The TV's wires run down through the wall cavity and in through the back panel of the console.

Entryways & Mudrooms

Even the smallest or sparest entryway to a home needs some kind of landing place, whether it's a bench with space underneath for a few boots and shoes, a modest peg rail for coats, or a full-blown mudroom with dedicated spaces for everyone in the household. In many homes, storage near the main entry door is necessary to keep muddy shoes and wet outerwear from being dragged into the living spaces. It's also the natural spot to drop off the car keys and set down the outgoing mail so you can pick it up on your way out. And in addition to its organizational function, a nicely appointed entryway is a welcome site to guests, providing them with an obvious place to hang their hat or drip-dry their wet umbrella.

Deciding what your entryways need is a simple matter of observation: who uses the entry most often, and what tends to collect on the floor just inside the door (or in the room nearest the entry)? Side and back doors used primarily by the family may have very different needs from a formal front entry used mostly by guests. Does the space have a coat rack so visitors can help themselves instead of having to wait for you to take their things? Do the kids' backpacks get dumped on the floor over a mess of shoes and pet supplies? Do your car keys and handbags end up cluttering the kitchen counters?

With a little forethought it's easy enough to figure out what's missing. Entryway storage solutions can be as simple as a few hooks for hanging gear and perhaps a side table for collecting odds and ends. More elaborate systems might include a series of cubbies, built-in seating, and a message board or calendar for managing daily traffic.

No mudroom? No problem. A simple collection of practical pieces can turn an empty entry into a highly functional storage space. You can buy complete ensembles ready-made, or mix and match pieces to suit your needs.

An empty alcove or nook can be the perfect opportunity for entryway storage. Here, a simple built-in provides a home for shoes or catch-all baskets, while drawers hold small miscellaneous items.

Front entries often call for a more formal arrangement of storage solutions. While perfectly functional and useful, these pieces complement the decorative styling of the home's living spaces.

Storage Cubes

The storage cube is a beautifully simple form, yet it is perhaps the most versatile of all modular home storage systems. Essentially a wooden box, the cube can hold anything you want it to, and you can build it almost any size you like. You can mount it on a wall, hang it from the ceiling, set it on a desk, or stack it on the floor with a group of other cubes. You can also add to its function with a coat hook or a shelf if it is wall hung.

Storage cubes are not a new idea, and you can certainly find a range of prefabricated versions made of a few different sizes and materials. But what's nice about building your own is that you get exactly what you want—in terms of size, shape, color, and add-ons. Maybe you'll build a series of square cubes for a cool twist on a standard bookcase or display shelving. Or maybe a long, shallow cube to hold spice jars in the kitchen. The photos below and on the facing page suggest a few more ways to customize your cubes.

The instructions on pages 130 to 131 show you the basic construction steps for building a square cube, both with and without a back panel. The material used here is finish-grade plywood. The same building techniques will work for rectangular cubes and for different materials, such as solid 1× lumber or MDF (medium-density fiberboard). Also, if you don't own a router but you have access to a table saw, the saw will work just as well for cutting rabbets.

Tools & Materials ▸

Wood gloves	Sander
Eye protection	Level
Circular saw	Wood glue
Straightedge guide	Finish-grade plywood
Router and	(¼", ¾")
straight bits	1" finish nails
Clamps	Keyhole hanger plates
Nail set	Hollow-wall anchors
Drill	Panhead screws
Hammer	Finishing materials
Chisel	

These storage cubes are hard at work in an entryway, providing each family member with a place for coats and other items they want to leave by the door.

More Ideas for Storage Cubes

Mix and match cubes of different shapes and sizes to create unique storage and display units.

A fixed shelf adds storage capacity and versatility to larger cubes. Install a shelf during assembly, setting the ends into dadoes cut into the cube's sides.

Large wall-mounted cubes can be a sleek and space-saving alternative to traditional bedside tables and other furniture pieces.

Matching cubes are conveniently modular. When you need more storage space, just add another cube.

How to Build Storage Cubes

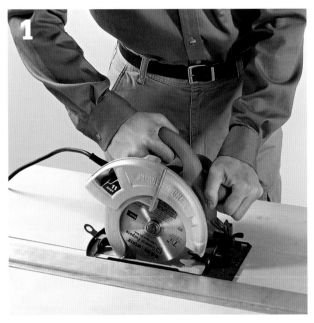

Cut the cube pieces to width using a circular saw and edge guide or a table saw. The width equals the depth of the finished cube. Cut two of these pieces to length, equal to the outside dimensions of the cube; these are the side pieces. Cut two more pieces for the top and bottom ½" shorter than the outside cube dimensions.

Mill a ½ × ¾" rabbet into both ends of the side pieces using a router with an edge guide or a router table. Make the cuts in several passes of increasing depth using a straight bit. You can save time by ganging the pieces together and routing each end with one setup.

Option: If you want the cube to have a back panel, mill ⁵⁄₁₆"-wide × ¼"-deep dado grooves into all four side pieces at least ¼" from the back edges. Cut the back panel to fit from ¼" plywood. Slide the panel in place during the side assembly.

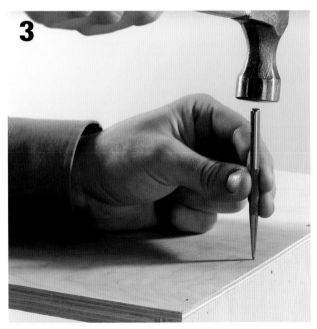

Dry-fit the cube parts to make sure the joints are tight and the cube is square. Assemble the cube with wood glue and 1" finish nails, driving the nails through the side pieces and into the ends of the top and bottom. Drive the nail heads just below the surface with a fine-pointed nail set.

Clamp the sides of the cube as soon as it is assembled, making sure the cube is perfectly square. You can use standard clamps perpendicular to the sides or strap clamps around the perimeter. After the glue has cured, sand and finish the cube as desired.

To wall-mount your cube, use keyhole hanger plates mortised into the rear side edges so the cube hangs flush to the wall. Hold each plate in position and trace along the edges of the keyhole. Mark the top and bottoms of the plate onto the back of the panel for use as cutting lines.

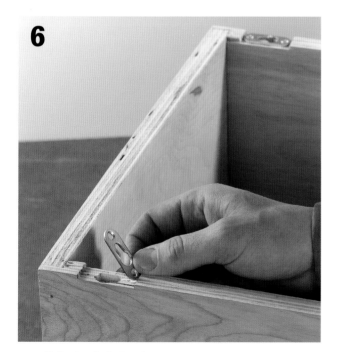

Install the keyhole hardware. Drill out the keyhole area using a bit that matches the large part of the keyhole. Then chisel a mortise inside the perimeter outline to the same depth as the hanger plate. Fasten the plate with screws. Hang the cube with heavy-duty panhead screws driven into wall studs or hollow-wall anchors.

Tool Tip ▸

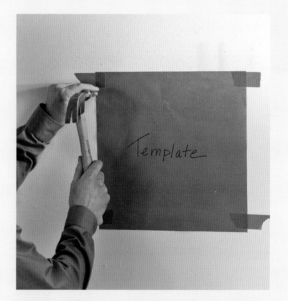

A paper drilling template makes it easy to get the holes right with keyhole hangers. Align a piece of paper with the top of the cube, then mark the center of each keyhole slot. Hold the paper so it's level on the wall and tap a nail at each marked point.

Suspended Shelving

When it comes to basic storage and display shelving, you're never short on options. You can choose from adjustable shelf systems with metal tracks, shelves that fit into corners, cantilevered shelves, cable-hung shelves, and, of course, the standard plank-and-bracket variety. But here's a shelf design you probably haven't thought of, and you certainly won't find kits for it at the local home center (although you can get all of the necessary parts there): it's a simple wooden shelf suspended at one or more corners by a length of threaded rod, or all-thread.

This suspended shelf not only looks cool, it's also a lot more versatile than pretty much anything else out there. Because this system relies on the ceiling for support, your shelves can extend almost any distance from the wall. Standard brackets, by contrast, allow for only about 12" of extension. An all-thread shelf can also hang independently of a wall, so it can go anywhere, much like cable-hung shelving. But unlike cable systems, all-thread shelves are rigid and thus more secure than cables, which can swing if bumped into. Better still, the parts for all-thread shelves are much less expensive than the specialty hardware needed for cable-hung shelving.

On the following pages, you'll learn the basic techniques for building and hanging a fully suspended shelf. The photos on page 135 show how to install shelves that hang from the wall, as well as large corner shelves that would be impractical to do with brackets. From there, you can adapt the all-thread system to create custom shelves in almost any location. As you'll see in the construction steps, all you need is a ceiling joist or two, and you can hang a shelf.

Tools & Materials ▸

Work gloves	Finishing tools
Eye protection	¾" finish-grade
Stud finder	plywood (or other
Circular saw and	shelf material)
straightedge guide	Scrap lumber
Router	Finish nails
Drill	Wood screws
Hammer	Finishing materials
Ladder	All-thread rod
Clamps	Hanger bolts
Portable drill guide	Coupling nuts
Hacksaw	Flat washers
Socket wrench	Hex nuts
Level	
Sander	

This custom suspended shelving hangs from ceiling joists, so it's strong, rigid, and can go almost anywhere. You can even adjust shelf heights simply by moving the supporting nuts on the all-thread. Ceiling-suspended shelving works nicely over breakfast bars, kitchen islands, and short partition walls.

How to Install Suspended Shelving

Locate the ceiling joists in the area using a stud finder or a finish nail and hammer. Mark both edges of each joist you will hang your shelf from. Plan to support ¾" plywood shelves at least every 32". Other materials may require closer spacing of supports.

Cross brace

Option: If you have attic access to the tops of the joists, you can use 2 × 4 crossbraces for more flexibility with support placement. Run the all-thread up through the ceiling surface and crossbraces (see step 7 on page 135) and anchor it with a nut and washer. Make sure the all-thread hangs plumb, then fasten the braces to the joists with screws.

Cut the shelf (or shelves) to size so it extends beyond the support locations by about 1¼" or so in each direction. Use a circular saw with an edge guide or a table saw to ensure straight cuts.

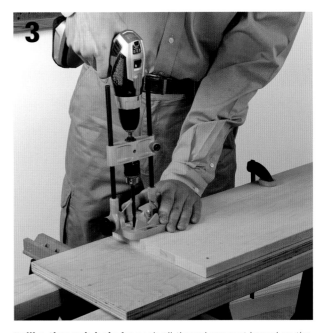

Drill a through-hole for each all-thread support based on the locations of the supporting joists. Then drill corresponding pilot holes through the ceiling surface and into the joists for the hanger bolts. *Tip: You can use the drilled shelf as a template for marking the ceiling holes.*

(continued)

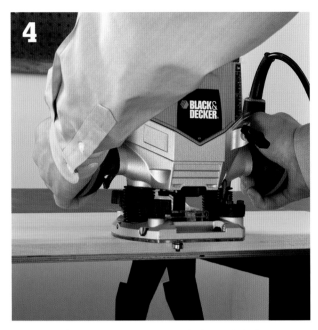

Sand and finish the shelf as desired. Plywood shelves look good with a slight roundover made with a router. For a melamine-veneered shelf, cover all cut edges with matching edge tape.

Drive the coarse-thread hanger bolt (see inset detail) end into a joist at each support location, keeping the bolt as plumb as possible. *Tip: Thread a coupling nut over the machine-thread end of the bolt and use a socket wrench to drive the bolt.*

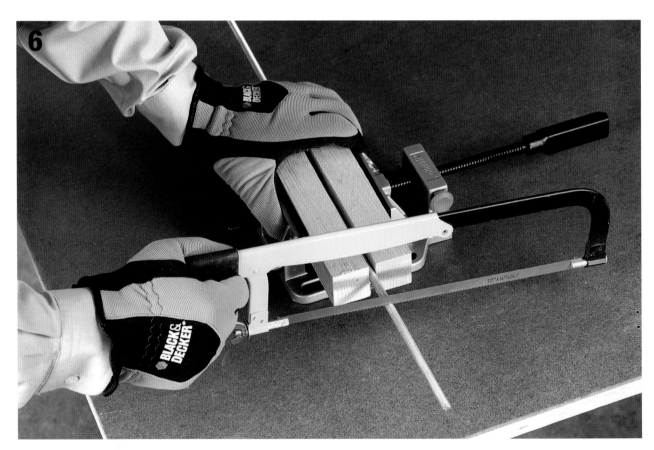

Cut the all-thread supports to length using a hacksaw. When measuring for length, be sure to account for the shelf thickness and the supporting nut and washer beneath the shelf. Plan for a little wiggle room inside the coupling nut for making adjustments.

7

Thread coupling nuts over the hanger bolts, then thread in the ends of the all thread. Slip the shelf over the bottom ends of the all thread and secure it with washers and nuts (additional washers and nuts on top of the shelf are optional). Level the shelf by adjusting the all-thread in the coupling nuts as needed.

8

To install suspended shelving against a wall, draw a level line on the wall representing the bottom face of the shelf. Fasten cleats (cut from 1 × 2 lumber; strips of shelf material; or ¾" quarter-round molding, as shown here) to the wall studs with trimhead screws or finish nails. Suspend the front edge of the shelf with all-thread supports. Once the shelf is in place, fasten it to the cleats with finish nails or screws.

9

For capacious yet streamlined corner shelves, use the techniques described in step 8 to install cleats along the wall. Cut the shelves square and support their free corners with a single length of all-thread following the techniques shown on page 134. *Tip: If you're using corner shelves for electronics or home office equipment, bore holes in an inconspicuous area of the shelves before you install them. Use the holes for running power cords and connecting cables.*

Mudroom Wall System

Even if your home doesn't have an actual mudroom, chances are the area closest to the main entry door (the one you use the most) is put to work just like a mudroom. It's where everything gets dropped off on the way into the house and where things are set so they're not forgotten on the way out. Ideally, a storage system here not only provides a proper place for hanging coats and leaving the car keys, it also helps organize the household's activity schedule.

Inspired by busy households everywhere, this easy-to-build mudroom wall is part storage system and part command center: deep wall cubbies provide space for stowing sports and outdoor gear; a long coat rack keeps jackets and tote bags out of the main part of the house; two wire baskets manage mail; small hooks hold car keys; and a shelf above the coat rack manages miscellaneous items like cell phones and sunglasses. Centrally located at eye level (so as not to be missed by harried commuters), a dry erase calendar manages daily activities, while a combination bulletin/message board allows for important notes.

All of the pieces in this mudroom wall system are available for purchase, so this project can be a completely plug-and-play affair. However, you might have a hard time finding an extralong coat rack that fits just right, so we've included steps for building that from scratch. Keep in mind that you can change the dimensions, placement, and arrangement of anything to suit your needs and your space.

Tools & Materials ▸

Work gloves	Lumber (1 × 4, 1 × 6)
Eye protection	2¼" finish nails
Hammer	2" wood screws
Stud finder	2½" coarse-thread
Pencil	drywall screws
Straightedge	Wall-mountable
Sandpaper	storage cubes
Shelf support brackets	Dry erase calendar
Wood putty or plugs	Bulletin board
Shoe containers	Wall-mountable
Shelf kit	pouches (2)
Graph paper	Wood plaque or
Tape measure	1 × 4 lumber
4 ft. level	Key hooks
Circular saw	Coat hooks
Router and roundover	Hollow-wall anchors
bit (optional)	(as needed)
Drill	Finishing materials
Wood glue	

A multipurpose storage and information system helps manage everything and everyone coming in and going out. And with this system you don't need a dedicated mudroom space—any wall area near the most-used entry door will do.

How to Install a Mudroom Wall System

Draw a scaled plan of your wall system on graph paper: Measure the available wall space and transfer those dimensions to the paper. Then, using scaled dimensions for each item, experiment with different spacing and arrangements. Create a final measured drawing to guide the rest of the installation.

Transfer the final layout to the wall using a laser level or a 4-ft. level. Make light pencil marks to represent the edges of each item. Use a hammer and finish nail or a stud finder to locate and mark all wall studs in the project area.

Cut two 1 × 6s to the desired length for the coat rack mounting board and shelf; make the shelf 1" or so longer than the mounting board for a decorative overhang at each end. Round over the edges of the shelf with a router or sandpaper.

Assemble the shelf. Fasten the shelf to the mounting board with glue and 2¼" finish nails so the pieces are flush at the back. Add a support bracket at each end using glue and 2" wood screws driven through the mounting board and finish nails driven through the shelf. You can use precut brackets or make your own from 1× or 2× lumber.

(continued)

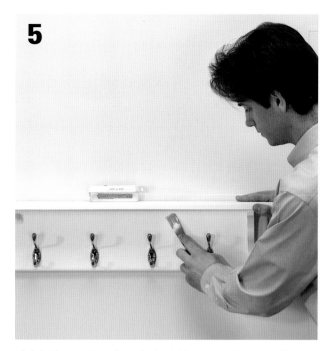

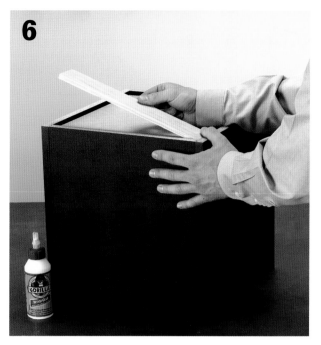

Finish the coat rack as desired. Mount coat hooks to the mounting board with even spacing. Fasten the rack to the wall with pairs of 2½" drywall screws at each stud location. Cover the screw heads with wood putty or plugs and touch up the finish.

Mount the storage cubes as directed by the manufacturer. Here, a wood mounting strip is being installed at the top rear edge of the cube to create a stronger nailing strip. Fasten mounting hardware to wall studs whenever possible. Otherwise, use heavy-duty hollow-wall anchors. *Option: To build your own storage cubes, see pages 130 to 131.*

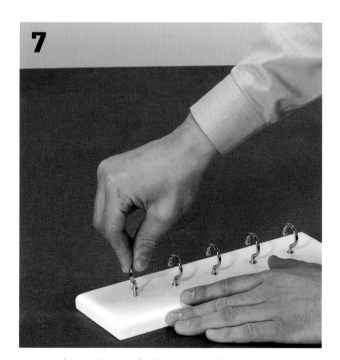

Create the car key rack. Finish a premilled wood plaque or a custom-cut piece of 1 × 4 or 1 × 6; mount key hooks or cup hooks using even spacing. Install the rack with screws driven into wall studs or anchors, and then hide the screw heads as with the coat rack.

Install the mail pouches, dry erase calendar, and bulletin board as directed by the manufacturers. If desired, add more functional pieces to your mudroom area, such as an umbrella stand, a coat tree for very long coats or to use for guests, or a small bench for putting on and removing shoes.

9

Substitute wire storage cubes for one or more of the solid-sided cubes. The wire mesh is great for airing out sports equipment and for drying wet gloves and hats. Mount the cubes to the wall with metal clips or short pieces of pipe-hanging tape (metal hanger strap).

10

A shoe cubby or shoe-and-boot rack helps minimize clutter along the floor. Shoe containers come in a huge range of types and sizes, and some can be wall mounted. For an entryway, choose a material that can stand up to wet and muddy shoes and boots.

11

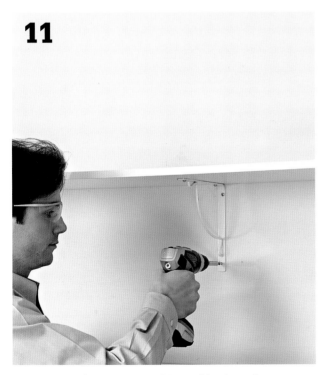

Install a shelf along the top of the wall in place of a top row of cubbies. Cubbies are great for keeping each person's stuff in one place, while a deep, high shelf is good for seasonal storage. Keep things neat with attractive baskets labeled with their contents.

12

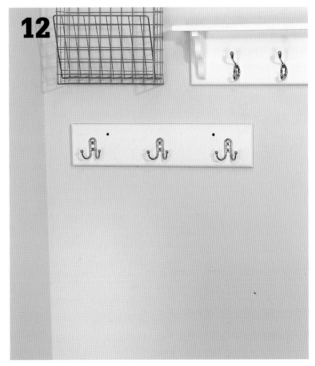

Add a low coat rack so children can be in charge of their own things. Mount a few of the same coat hooks used in the main rack to a painted 1 × 4, then screw the board to the wall studs, or use hollow-wall anchors.

Underststairs Bookcases

If your home has a staircase with open space below, chances are you've wondered how to make the most of that oddly configured square footage. This bookcase project could be the answer. Behind the two pairs of gently rising birch-frame doors you'll find a bank of birch plywood shelves that are designed for use as a formal bookcase. Because the door panels are created with Plexiglas, the shelves are also quite suitable for display purposes.

While the bookcase cabinets must be custom-fit to your space, the basic design of the individual units is quite simple. Each cabinet is essentially a plywood box with an angled top. The boxes fit side by side in the understairs area, flush with the wall surfaces. The shelves in each unit incorporate birch 1 × 2 shelf edge to improve their appearance and stiffen the shelf boards.

A birch face frame is wrapped around the perimeter of the project, concealing the plywood edges. The swinging doors are also made of birch. The secret to building the face frames and the door frames is a clever woodworking technique known as the pocket screw joint made with angled screws driven into the back sides of the mating pieces.

Understairs storage units are often made with slide-out shelving or pull-out drawers. This strategy allows for efficient use of space since the pull-out units can be nearly as deep as the total stair width. The drawback is that the drawers or slide-out shelves can be a bit rickety, especially if you're not an experienced cabinetmaker. When designing your project, you can increase the storage space by deepening the shelves and using them as storage cubbies. If your staircase is bounded by another interior wall, you can add a bookcase on the other side, with the two bookcases sharing a divided panel or wall.

A rich formal bookcase inhabits the previously wasted space underneath a staircase. The books are protected by birch doors with Plexiglas panels that have a soft, contemporary design feeling.

Tools & Materials ▸

Tools

Work gloves
Eye protection
Respirator
Stud finder
Level
Pencil
Utility knife or wallboard saw
Pry bar
Drill
Router (and rabbet bit)
Pilot bits
Chisel
Large pipe clamps
Framing square
Table saw
Pneumatic brad nailer
HVLP sprayer (optional)
Hammer
Nail set

Materials

2 × 4 lumber
Plywood stock (¼", ¾")
Wood glue
Brads
150- or 220-grit sandpaper
Desired finish
Pocket screws
6d finish nails
1¼" drywall screws
Coarse-thread drywall screws
Wood putty; frosted glass
Plexiglas

Glazier's points
Latches
Pulls
1 × 2 hardwood
Shims
Hinges

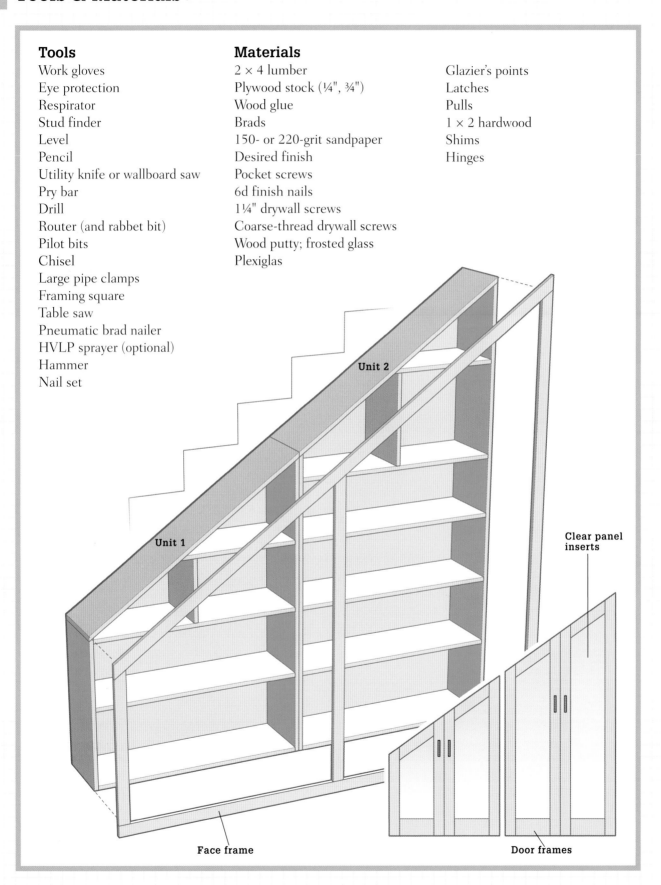

Unit 2

Unit 1

Clear panel inserts

Face frame

Door frames

How to Build the Understairs Bookcase

1

Lay out the planned project on the walls. Be sure to identify and label all stud locations as well as any wiring, plumbing or ductwork in the project area. Try to plan the opening in the wall so it will be bordered by existing studs, and with the wall covering cut up to the studs but not beyond.

2

Cut and remove the wall covering with electrical service. First shut off electricity at the main service panel. To minimize dust, use a utility knife or wallboard saw to cut the wall covering along the cutting lines. Pry off the wall covering, taking care not to damage surrounding walls surfaces.

3

Install 2 × 4 sleepers on the floor after you've thoroughly cleaned up the project area and disposed of all debris properly. Sleepers should butt against the wall's sole plate and run back in a perpendicular fashion slightly further than the planned project depth. Install a sleeper at the end of the project area, beneath the midpoint, and at 16" intervals.

4

Rip plywood stock into strips for making the cabinet frame and shelves. We used ¾" birch-veneer plywood to match the birch that is used for the face frame and door frames. The cabinet frame pieces are ripped to 12" wide but the shelves should be only 11¼" wide to allow for the ¾"-thick shelf edge strips. Cut all parts to length.

5

Assemble the unit frames with wood glue and coarse-thread drywall screws driven through the outer faces and into the edges of the mating boards. Drill countersunk pilot holes for the screws. Work on a flat surface and check the joint with a framing square to make sure they are square. If you have large pipe clamps, use them to clamp the workpieces before driving the screws. Make both the Unit 1 and Unit 2 frames (tops, sides, and bottom panels).

6

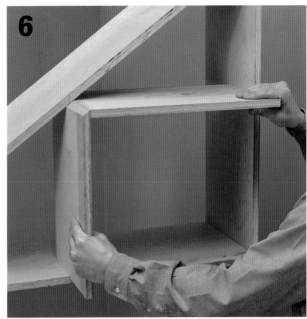

Install shelf boards in the cabinet frame. The shelves should be flush with the back edges of the frame, leaving a ¾" reveal in the front. Draw shelf layout lines on both faces of the frame pieces so you can center the screws. Install the full-width shelves first. Assemble the shorter shelves and their divider supports into L shapes, and then install them as a unit. Cut back panels from ¼" plywood and attach them with brads.

7

Attach hardwood shelf edge to the shelves and the divider support edges. The tops of the 1 × 2 edge boards should be flush with the top surfaces of the shelves. The vertical edging pieces should be flush with the outside edges of the dividers.

8

Apply a finish to the cabinet units. Sand all wood surfaces with 150- or 220-grit sand paper, wipe down with mineral spirits, and then apply two to three light coats of water-based polyurethane. We used an HVLP sprayer to apply the finish, but wipe-on polyurethane works just fine if you don't have spraying equipment.

(continued)

Closet Office

When you need a dedicated office space and don't have a den or an extra bedroom available, the conventional option is to set up shop in some other room, such as the living room. But sharing a space has its drawbacks. Busy living spaces aren't always conducive to work. On the flip side, office equipment and file storage aren't exactly dazzling décor for living spaces. Office areas that aren't well defined also tend to collect other kinds of paperwork or, worse, general household clutter.

A good option for your new office space just might be a closet. Tucked away in its own discreet nook, a closet office is nicely contained and clearly separated from other activities. The office itself requires no extra living space—all you need is a little room for a chair when you're working at the desk. Perhaps best of all, the office and all of its contents are out of sight (and mind) as soon as you close the closet doors. This office design is simple and easy to build yet provides all of the necessary basics for both tasks and storage in a modern work space.

Tools & Materials ▸

Work gloves
Eye protection
Caulk gun
Circular saw and
    straightedge guide
Level
Drill with bits
Hacksaw
Wrench
Sander
Stud finder
Hammer
Clamps
Construction adhesive
Hardwood-veneer
    MDF-core plywood
    (finish-grade on
    one side) (¼", ¾")

Finish nails (1¼", 2")
3½" wood screws
2¼" trimhead screws
⁵⁄₁₆" all-thread rod
Hanger bolts
Coupling nuts
Flat washers
Hex nuts
Hardwood lumber
    (1 × 1, 1 × 2)
¾" particleboard with
    plastic laminate
    (on one side) for
    desktop
Wood glue
1¼" coarse-thread
    drywall screws
Finishing materials

Closets are prime real estate in any home, but if you can manage to clear one out, you can create a private, efficient office space that's instantly hidden behind closed doors.

How to Transform a Closet Into an Office

Power ▸

Provide electrical service to your office by branching off of an existing circuit. Here, boxes for a light fixture and a wall receptacle were added and wired to a room circuit. Patches for the drywall cut to route the wiring will be hidden by the panel and don't need a complete finish.

1

Prepare the walls for the paneling by removing any baseboard or other moldings. Make sure the wall is smooth and dust free. Locate and mark the wall studs to guide the installation; the panel seams should fall over stud centers.

Option: If you will panel the ceiling, locate the ceiling joists in the closet, and then map out their locations onto paper. The joists will support the suspended bookshelves, and it would be difficult to locate the joists once the paneling is up. If you're not paneling the ceiling, find and mark the joists after step 6 on page 148.

2

Finish the good side of the paneling stock as desired. Cut the first panel to length, cutting from the back side with a circular saw to prevent splintering. Apply beads of construction adhesive to the back of the panel, and press the panel against the wall so the side edges are centered over studs.

(continued)

3

Adjust the panel so it's perfectly plumb, then nail it to the wall studs with 1¼" finish nails. Use the nails sparingly; you need only enough to ensure the panel stays flat and the edges are securely and evenly adhered.

4

Cut and install the remaining panels. Use the straight factory edges for the butted seams. At the inside corners, place the second (perpendicular) panel with its factory edge butted against the first panel. If the seams are tight, you don't need to hide them with molding.

5

Plan the bookshelf spacing as desired, then draw level lines onto the walls to represent the bottom edge of each shelf. Cut and install 1 × 1 shelf cleats so their top edges are flush with the level lines. Fasten the cleats with 2¼" trimhead screws driven into wall studs.

6

Cut the shelves from ¾" plywood. The top and middle shelves are L-shaped, 11" deep along the back wall, with an 18"-long, full-depth leg at one end. The bottom shelf matches the leg dimensions. If desired, drill a hole near the back corner of each shelf for routing power cords.

7

Drill holes for the all-thread hangers following the ceiling joist layout. Finish the shelves as desired. Install the shelves using the techniques shown on pages 134 to 135.

8

Draw level lines to represent the top edges of the desktop cleats: these are 1½" below the desk surface. *Tip: Standard desktop height is 29 to 30" from the floor, while typing surfaces are typically 26 to 27".* Cut and install the 1 × 2 cleats flush with the lines using a 3½" wood screw driven into each wall stud.

9

Cut two identical pieces of desktop stock to fit the closet dimensions, with a little bit of wiggle room for getting it in place (be sure to account for the ¾" thickness of the 1 × 2 nosing). Glue the pieces together on their bare faces using wood glue and a few 1¼" screws to clamp them together while the glue dries. Make sure the pieces are perfectly flush at their front edges.

10

Install the desktop. If desired, drill a large hole (1½"-dia. or so) through the desktop for routing cords. Cut, sand, and finish 1 × 2 stock for the decorative nosing. Install the nosing with wood glue and 2" finish nails, keeping it flush with the desk surface. Set the desktop onto the cleats; its weight will keep it securely in place.

Kids' Stackable Storage Blocks

If you are looking for a multipurpose storage project that is easy to build and usable in any room, stackable storage blocks are the answer. Made from finish-grade ¾" birch plywood, the size, color, and style of these blocks are easy to adapt to any space. If you plan to stack the blocks, install the optional 1 × 3 slats to hold each block safely in place. Be creative. The possibilities are endless.

Finishing Your Blocks ▶

There is something about boxes that gets kids excited, as any parent can attest who has purchased an expensive new toy for their child only to see it set aside in favor of the packaging. The simple wood boxes in the project are plenty fascinating for kids all by themselves, but you can still build on that fun by finishing the boxes in interesting and colorful ways. Here are a couple of suggestions:

- Make cutouts in the side in familiar shapes such as starts, crescent moons, or simple animal forms.
- Find some large stencils and paint letters on the faces of the cubes so they look like building blocks.
- Paint each face of the cube a different bright color, while choosing a single tone for all of the interior surfaces.

Stackable blocks provide a storage option that is also kid friendly and big fun.

Tools, Materials & Cutting List ▸

Tools

Work gloves
Eye Protection
Circular saw with
    plywood blade
Drill with bits
Utility knife
Straightedge guide
Sander

Materials

¾" birch plywood
1 × 3" pine
Wood screws
   (#6 × 1½, 1¼)
Finishing materials

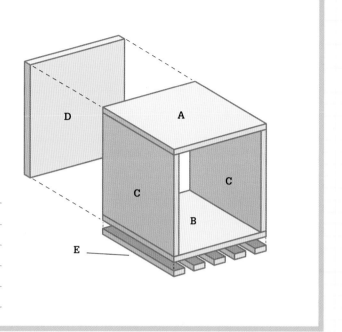

Key	Part	Dimension
A	(1) Top	¾ × 21¾ × 21" birch plywood
B	(1) Bottom	¾ × 21¾ × 21" birch plywood
C	(1) Sides	¾ × 21¾ × 22½" birch plywood
D	(1) Back	¾ × 22½ × 22½" birch plywood
E	(9) Slats	¾ × 2½ × 22½" pine

How to Build Storage Blocks

Lay out the block pieces. Score all crosscuts along the cutting line with a utility knife to help minimize tearout, and then cut the pieces to size.

Fasten the top and bottom to the sides, spacing countersunk wood screws approximately every 5". Add the back panel and attach the wood cleats to the underside of the bottom panel with 1¼" wood screws. Fill screw holes, sand well, and finish as desired.

Crown Molding Shelves

Here's a neat trick: build a shelf that stores, displays, and elevates your favorite collectibles and knickknacks so they're well within sight but safely out of the way. Before building this crown molding shelf, one skill you may wish to brush up on is cutting and coping crown molding. Working with crown molding requires some mental gymnastics, but once you learn the floor routine you'll be glad you did. You can hang your new shelves at just about any height, although they naturally look more comfortable higher up on the wall. At least try and position them at or slightly above eye level. Locating the shelves so the bottom edge rests on top of a door head casing is one good strategy.

This crown molding shelf is essentially a built-up box in a straight run along one wall. There are also different variations on how the shelf can be installed. For example, you can wrap the entire room with it, simply span from one wall to another, or place it on three walls only. The design is flexible to suit different needs and tastes. And by choosing trim types and styles that already are present in your home you can enhance the built-in look. If you have the woodworking equipment and skills, consider using dado joints instead of butt joints where it makes sense. With dado joints, the wood parts can expand and contract (as they are prone to) without creating separation gaps.

Fashioned from crown molding and dimension lumber, this elegant shelf fits above a door or along the top of a wall to provide new display space for knickknacks and your favorite collections.

Tools, Materials & Cutting List ▶

Tools
Work gloves
Eye protection
Table saw
Miter saw
Hammer
Level or laser level
Drill/driver and bits
Tape measure
Square
Sander
Caulk gun

Materials
4" Drywall or deck
  screws
Crown molding
Panel adhesive

Pine or oak lumber
  (1×, 2×)
Finish nails
Finishing materials

Part	Desc.	No.	Size	Material
A	Shelf top	1	¾ × 7" × length	Pine or oak
B	Shelf bottom	1	¾ × 2¾" × length	Pine or oak
C	Shelf front	1	¾ × 4½" × length	Pine or oak
D	Crown	1*	¾ × 4¼" × length	Crown molding
E	Ledger	1	1½ × 3½" × length	2 × 4
F	Filler (opt.)	1 or 2	¾ × 2¾ × 3½"	Pine or oak

* Make mitered return if end of shelf is open

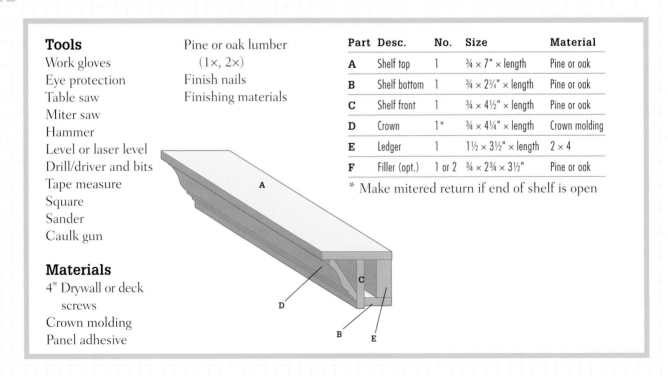

How to Build a Crown Molding Shelf

1

Attach the ledger to the wall studs with 4" screws and panel adhesive. Double-check to make sure the ledger is level after you drive the first screw. *Tip: Use a laser level to create a level reference line for the shelf ledger installation.*

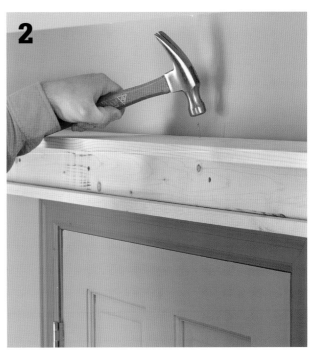

2

Attach the bottom strip to the ledger board with panel adhesive and wood screws, and then attach the shelf to the top of the ledger, making sure the ends are flush with the ends of the bottom strip.

3

Attach wood spacers to the front face of the ledger to align the front panel when it is pressed against the spacers. Then attach the front panel by nailing it to the bottom strip first, and then driving finish nails through the top panel.

4

Finally, nail the crown molding in place at 12" intervals. Sand and finish as desired.

Stock-Cabinet Hobby Center

If you or someone in your family enjoys a hobby or activity, whether it's computing, scrapbooking, drawing, or anything else that involves pleasant time seated and engaged in your vocation, you deserve to have a special place set aside for that activity. And here, it is important to note, *set aside* does not mean "spread out on the kitchen table between family meals." A dedicated spot with loads of storage, a pleasing appearance, and an efficient footprint can all be obtained with this corner hobby center which provides the things you need to spend time on your activity, not manage it.

In this corner hobby center, upper and lower cabinets are combined to deliver excellent and attractive storage options. At the same time, some on-site carpentry creates a stable frame for a spacious but not overpowering L-shaped desk. The laminate desktop configuration provides not just room to spread out a project or stage supplies left and right, but also provides three access points (center, left, and right) for you to either move around a large project or for others to pull up a chair and help or just watch.

Tools & Materials ▸

Work gloves	Corner cabinet
Eye protection	Countertop
Level or laser level	Drywall or deck
Tape measure	screws
Drill/driver	Wood screws
Stud finder	Lighting equipment
Tape	(optional)
Clamps	Finish nails
Circular saw	Finishing materials
Miter saw	Lumber (2 × 2,
Base cabinets (2)	2 × 3, 2 × 4)
Upper cabinets (2)	¾" plywood

Stock kitchen cabinets can be used effectively in any room in your house. Here, a pair of base cabinets, two upper cabinets, and a corner cabinet are fashioned together with a custom laminate countertop to make a very useful hobby/craft center.

How to Create a Stock-Cabinet Hobby Center

Use a level or laser level to create the level line at the desired height (here, 52½" above the floor). Also find and mark wall stud locations in the installation area. Fasten a temporary ledger board for the upper cabinets just below the level line.

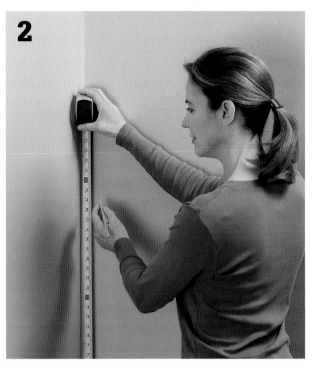

Extend your tape in the corner and make height marks for the tops of the base cabinets (here, 34½").

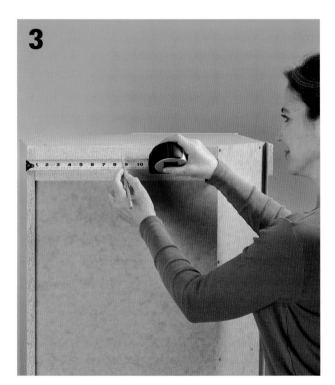

Transfer the stud locations to the wall cabinet backs and then to the inside surfaces.

Fasten the upper cabinet to the wall studs to hold it in place, but do not drive the screws all the way (this allows for a little fine-tuning).

(continued)

5

Before fully sinking wall screws, be sure the front of all wall cabinets are flush. Make adjustments as necessary to get them flush, clamp, predrill, then fasten.

6

Position the base cabinets at the layout lines and fasten them to wall studs with screws driven through the back nailing strips of the cabinets and into the walls at stud locations.

7

Install 2 × 2 cleats for the back corner of the desktop, just below the level line for the base cabinet tops, driving screws at wall stud locations.

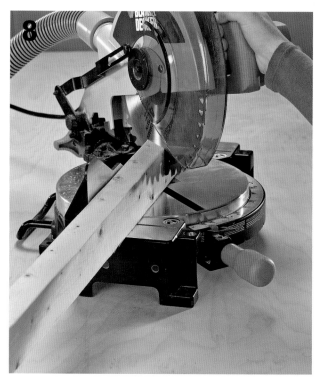

8

Cut a diagonal ledger brace with opposing miters to fit between the two wall cleats and provide extra support for the desktop.

Fasten the diagonal brace to the wall cleats with wood screws. Trim the angles of the brace where it meets the cleats as needed so it fits flush against the cleats.

With a helper, position the desktop on the cabinet tops and cleats. You can make the desktop yourself from a layer of particleboard with buildup strips below, finished with plastic laminate, or have a custom top made at a cabinet shop.

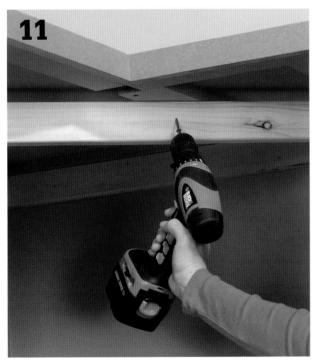

Attach the desktop by driving screws up through the wall cleats and brace—if there is no buildup strip between the brace and the desktop, cut a strip of ¾" plywood and insert it as a filler strip between the parts.

Add task lighting and convenient electrical receptacles according to your skill and comfort level with wiring.

Basements, Attics & Garages

In addition to being the best places for messy work and other creative pursuits, the unfinished spaces of our homes are great for storing things we don't use very often.

This chapter is all about finding the right solutions to making your unfinished spaces satisfy both your storage needs and the everyday uses they're intended for, like sheltering your car. And there's probably a lot more storage space there than you think. Often a few simple products are all you need to claim stowaway space in previously ignored areas, such as the ceiling space in the garage or the unfinished floor surface in the attic.

Weeding out excess clutter will certainly save you time and money in the long run, and will make your final storage plan simpler and more manageable. It's also important to take stock of your items, to make sure they're stored safely. For example, mildew-prone things like books and documents don't belong in a damp basement environment, while temperature-sensitive items can alternately freeze and wither in an unfinished attic.

In this chapter:

- Storage Strategies
- Laundry Center
- Basement Stairway Shelving
- Joist Shelves
- Basement Storage Wall
- Utility Shelves
- Garage Deck
- Adjustable Shelving
- Garage Cabinets
- Garage Ceiling Storage
- Attic Storage Deck

Storage Strategies

Custom shelving in the basement can be strictly utilitarian or it can have a more finished look. This practical shelf system anchors the uprights to the ceiling joists above, giving the top shelves several more inches of headroom.

Basements and garages are nice, big, boxy spaces just full of opportunity for storage—or so it seemed before you moved into your house and started filling them up to the brim. But don't worry; there's still hope. It just takes some careful planning and a little ingenuity to fit all the puzzle pieces into an organized picture.

Attic spaces come in all shapes and sizes and might be anything but boxy. Some are framed with rafters and offer a lot of empty floor space (but first you'll need a floor), while others are built with trusses that may or, more likely, may not leave you much room to stash boxes, let alone to move your body through to get to the stuff. The following tips will help get you rolling toward a workable storage plan, regardless of your particular space constraints.

Basements

The main considerations for basic utility storage in the basement are how to keep items organized and accessible and how to protect them from inhospitable conditions—namely flooding, condensation, and damp concrete surfaces. In an unfinished basement, simple utility shelving is the way to go. A sturdy set of lumber or steel shelves keeps everything off of the floor, where it's safe from minor sewer backups and groundwater flooding.

In general, the more shelves you can have, the better. More shelves make it easy to keep a variety of items organized without having to double-stack containers. Tall shelves let you store things right up to the ceiling (or floor joists) without creating precarious towers of boxes and bins. Good places to install shelving include bump-outs and alcoves that are too small for a workshop or recreation space, and open sections of walls that are away from the main traffic routes through the basement. Building a custom set of shelves under the stairs is a great way to steal some space in a small or already crowded basement.

In addition to shelving, you can utilize the open joist spaces for storing small items. Joists also make good anchors for a hanging wardrobe—a closet rod with a zip-up plastic cover. If your laundry facilities are in the basement, you can hang open closet rods from the joists for drip-drying clothes. A set of old kitchen cabinets and a counter surface can make the laundry area much more practical and livable.

With all basement storage, keep in mind that concrete floors and poured concrete or block foundation walls can be sources of moisture no matter how dry they feel to the touch. Masonry surfaces also emit salt residues along with moisture that can discolor clothing, paper, and many other materials. It's best to avoid direct contact with masonry altogether. Anything stored on the floor or against foundation walls should be kept inside sturdy plastic containers. However, if you live in a humid climate or your basement is often damp, provide some ventilation for plastic containers, or seal them up and add packets of silica gel or other drying agent to prevent condensation inside containers.

Not to be underestimated, the everyday functions of the home like cleaning and laundering are much more manageable with a dedicated work area. This could be as small as a closet with a double-stack washer/dryer unit or a small corner in the basement (as shown here). Consider a combination of shelves, drawers, and cabinets based on your needs.

Heavy-duty steel rivet shelving is inexpensive and strong and sets up in minutes. The rivet system that holds the shelves in place also makes them highly adjustable. Most units come with precut particleboard planks for the shelf surfaces.

Garages

The garage is home to so many different things—yard and garden equipment, bikes and sports gear, workshop tools and materials, and vehicles of all descriptions, not to mention overflow storage items from the house. Ideally, your garage storage strategy will create a place for each group of items while leaving enough room for your essential garage activities.

Once you've completed the dirty work of weeding out the junk and inventorying the stuff you're keeping, arrange everything by category and frequency of use. Plan to keep all of the gardening stuff in one place, the car maintenance supplies in another, etc., and plan to stow the seasonal and long-term items in the least convenient locations. Next, determine where, and how much, space is needed for everyday functions. For example, if there's not much room for opening the car doors, don't plan on crowding the side walls with floor-standing shelves or hanging tools. Instead, think about overhead shelving along the side walls and a tool organizer tucked into a corner. The goal is to utilize every available space without impeding movement or access to stored items. Here are some other options to consider:

- Most garages have relatively high ceilings, and this, combined with the dead space we leave open for parking vehicles, means that much of the garage area is available for overhead storage.
- Prefabricated racks are great for loading up with large plastic bins full of seasonal stuff.
- Pulley systems provide safe storage and easy access for unwieldy items like canoes, extension ladders, or even small trailers.
- Simple screw-in bike hooks are ideal for hanging bikes or just about anything else.
- A built-in storage deck or loft (see pages 184 to 189) adds considerable storage space without limiting parking areas; or, you can use the underdeck space for additional storage or a small work station.

Tip ▸

Better than a tennis ball on a string. Tight garage spaces leave little room for error when parking the car. Install a parking stop to ensure safe and accurate docking every time.

Complete garage units are sold as predesigned packages at home centers. They are available in many styles. This works well if you have the appropriate amount of space for the storage system. They often incorporate cabinets, shelving, baskets, and other accessories that can be mixed and matched depending on your needs.

Standards with brackets suitable for heavy weight are readily available at home centers. The tracks are screwed into wall studs (or hollow-wall anchors). All accessories snap into place anywhere along the track. Some tracks are suitable for slat walls and cabinets also (inset).

Attics

The best thing about attic storage spaces is that, unlike garages and some basements, attics generally don't serve any practical purpose, so it's totally "free" space. Large, open attics with sizable framing can offer hundreds of square feet of storage. And even if your attic is suitable for conversion to living space, you can still plan for ample storage space in the perimeter areas near the exterior walls.

However, one big question remains: Is your attic a good candidate for storage? If the roof is framed with rafters and the joists supporting the ceiling below are 2 × 8s or larger, the space might be ideal for a large storage deck and perhaps some shelving along the sides. On the other hand, if the roof is framed with trusses made with 2 × 4 lumber, the "floor" area is probably broken up with intersecting supports, and loading up what open spaces there are might result in a droopy ceiling in the rooms below (or worse). In any case, when in doubt, have the structure examined by a pro to learn what your options are.

That said, there are a few easy ways to turn an empty attic into a sizable cache for long-term storage. For wide-open attics, the best option is to install a floor deck, either of ½" plywood or lightweight plastic decking panels (see pages 198 to 201). Once you have a stable surface to work from, you can add some rudimentary shelves to claim additional space between the roof framing and the deck. Another good place for shelving is up against a gable wall at either end of the roof structure.

For those with less commodious, truss-framed attics, you can install a simple track system that lets you roll storage bins in and out through the interstices of the framing like coal cars in a mine. You can also create little mini-deck areas with plywood or plastic panels, perhaps connecting them with a catwalk path for access.

If your attic storage plan includes frequent trips to the new space, it might be worth the time and expense of installing an access ladder. Many of these are made for DIY installation (see page 201 for an installation overview).

Trusses are employed in most residential roof supports systems. They are strong and economical, but unfortunately they create impediments to storage. Still, it is possible to work around them, just be sure that you never cut them—not even a small notch.

Do not underestimate the storage capabilities of an attic. Here a reach-in closet is flanked by two built-in wall niches to take advantage of space regardless of the sloping ceiling.

Rafters take longer to install than trusses because they are hand-built one a time. They allow plenty of open space below for building storage decks or even converting your attic into living space.

Laundry Center

While there may be no scientific evidence to prove it, we all know that there's a direct correlation between the quality of a laundry room space and how much we dread doing the laundry. Cramped, cluttered, or poorly arranged rooms slow the work and add to it a general sense of unpleasantness. And things get complicated when you can't complete the laundry tasks in the laundry room—you have to hang up your sweaters to dry over the bathtub and do all the folding on the kitchen table.

If this sounds familiar, you'll be glad to know that it doesn't take much to turn an ordinary laundry area into an efficient storage and work center. Nor does it take a lot of space. The project shown here requires only about nine feet of wall area, including where the washer and dryer go. And with a few extra feet available on a nearby wall, you can add a hideaway ironing board that folds up into a recessed cabinet when not in use.

In addition to the space-saving ironing board, this project includes some practical features that could change the way you view laundry: washable laminated cabinets keep stored items dust free (great for stowing extra towels and linens, cleaning supplies, a sewing kit, etc.). Below one cabinet is a custom-built hanging shelf for holding detergent and stain removers within easy reach of the washer. A hanger rod between the cabinets accommodates dozens of drip-dry articles without getting in the way. And a full-depth, 4 feet long laminate countertop lets you fold clothes just a step from the dryer, while deep utility shelves below can store anything from laundry baskets to backup supplies from the wholesale store.

Tools & Materials ▸

Work gloves
Eye protection
4 ft. level
Drill
Circular saw and straightedge guide
Drywall saw
Plumb bob
Stud finder
Household iron
30"w × 24"h and 36"w × 30"h melamine-laminate wall cabinets
3½" heavy-duty wood screws
¾" melamine-covered particleboard (laminated on both sides)
Polyurethane glue
Coarse-thread drywall screws (1¼", 2")
Melamine-laminate edge tape and stickers
Hanger rod with mounting brackets
Lumber (1 × 2, 2 × 2)
Deck screws (3½", 2½")
2¼" finish nails
48"-long post-formed laminate countertop (straight section)
Countertop end cap kit
¾" particleboard
Wood glue
Ironing board cabinet for recessed wall mounting
Drop hook (optional)

What every laundry room needs: dedicated areas for ironing, hanging, folding, and stacking clothes, plus convenient spaces for holding point-of-use supplies and for stored items that you want to keep clean.

How to Create a Laundry Center

1

Mark the cabinet locations onto the wall, including level lines to represent the cabinets' top edges. Standard cabinet height is 84" above the floor, but make sure the washer door won't block with the hanging shelf. Locate and mark all of the wall studs behind the cabinet locations.

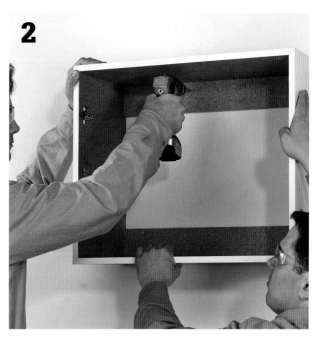

2

Assemble the cabinets, if necessary. Position each cabinet with its top edge flush to the level line, drill pilot holes, and fasten through the back panel and into the wall studs with at least four 3½" heavy-duty wood screws (or install according to the manufacturer's directions).

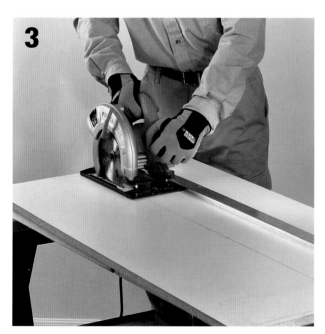

3

Cut pieces of ¾" melamine-covered particleboard for the hanging shelf. Cut the top and bottom pieces equal to the cabinet depth × the cabinet width minus 1½". Cut the side pieces equal to the cabinet depth × the overall shelf height (as desired). Cut the back panel equal to the cabinet depth × the shelf height minus 1½" in both directions.

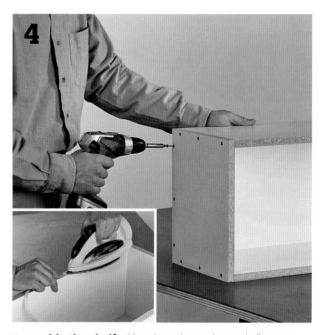

4

Assemble the shelf with polyurethane glue and 2" coarse-thread drywall screws or particleboard screws. Cover any exposed front edges and screw heads with melamine-laminate edge tape and cosmetic stickers (inset). When the glue has cured, mount the shelf to the bottom cabinet panel with 1¼" coarse-thread drywall screws driven through pilot holes.

(continued)

5

Mount the hanger rod to the sides of the cabinets using the provided screws. Locate the rod as close as possible to the front edge of the cabinets (without hindering door operation) and as high as you can comfortably reach.

6

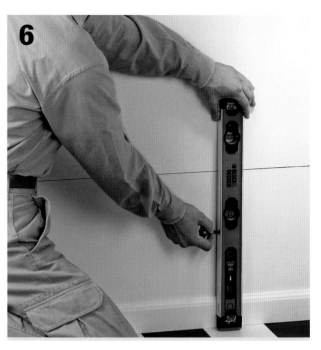

Mark the layout of the countertop and shelf unit onto the wall. Draw level lines at 34½" and at the desired height for the shelf top minus ¾". Draw plumb lines for the end panel at 46½ and 47¼" from the side wall and for the shelf support at 22⅞ and 23⅝" from the side wall. Also mark all wall studs in the area.

7

Following the layout lines, cut and install 2 × 2 wall cleats for the countertop along the back and side walls. Fasten the cleats to the wall studs with 3½" deck screws. Cut and install 1 × 2 cleats for the shelf, shelf support, and end panel using 2½" deck screws or drywall screws.

8

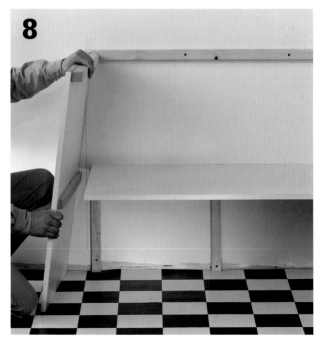

Build the end panel and shelf to size at 34½" long × the countertop depth minus ¾". Cut the shelf at 46½" long × the same width as the end panel. Add a 2 × 2 cleat flush with the top edge of the end panel. Fasten the shelf and end panel to the wall cleats with polyurethane glue and 2¼" finish nails. Fasten through the end panel and into the shelf edge with 2" screws.

Cut the shelf support to fit underneath the shelf. Notch the back edge to fit around the 1 × 2 wall cleat, then install the support to the cleat and shelf with glue and 2¼" finish nails.

Prepare the countertop by cutting a stiffener panel from ¾" particleboard to fit inside the edges on the underside of the countertop. Fasten the panel with wood glue and 1¼" screws. If desired, install an end cap kit onto the end opposite the side wall following the manufacturer's directions. Set the countertop in place and secure it to the 2 × 2 cleats with 2" screws.

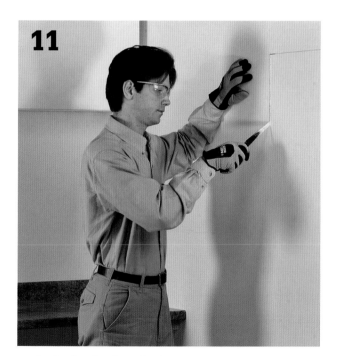

Begin the ironing board cabinet installation by locating two adjacent wall studs and drawing level lines to mark the top and bottom of the wall opening. Make sure there's no wiring or plumbing inside the wall cavity, then cut the drywall along the stud edges and the level lines using a drywall saw.

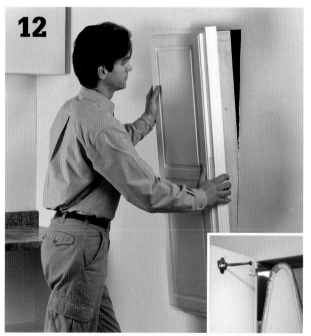

Fit the cabinet into the wall opening and secure it to the wall studs using the recommended screws. *Tip: Add a drop hook on the inside of the cabinet door for hanging up ironed clothes (inset). The hook drops down against the door when not in use.*

Basement Stairway Shelving

In many homes, the basement stairs offer two easy options for convenient and out-of-the-way storage. One utilizes the stud cavities along the stairwell wall. The other occupies that large yet awkward triangular area underneath the staircase. In both places, a simple lumber shelving system lets you take advantage of underused space without sacrificing valuable square footage.

Adding shelves along a stairwell wall couldn't be simpler. All it requires is notching a 2 × 6 shelf board to fit over the wall studs, then screwing the shelf in place. This gives you a 5½"-deep shelf space between the studs, plus a 2"-deep lip in front of each stud. Of course, the stairwell wall must be unfinished on one side for this type of shelving. If the stairwell wall isn't an option, perhaps you have an open wall in the basement or garage—any wall with exposed framing will work.

Utility shelves for the understairs space are made with a 2 × 4 support frame and plywood shelf surfaces. The stair structure itself provides support at one end of the shelves. Like the stud-wall shelves, you can set the understairs shelving at any height or spacing that you like. In the project shown on pages 169 to 171, the shelf system includes a low bottom shelf that's built with extra supports, good for keeping heavy items off of the basement floor.

Shelves along an open stairwell wall (left photo) can accommodate loads of smaller items. If your basement door is near the kitchen, these shelves are great for backup pantry storage. Shelves underneath the staircase (right photo) are ideal for basement workshop storage and for long pieces of lumber and other materials.

Tools & Materials ▸

For Stairway Shelves:

Work gloves	Circular saw
Eye protection	Mallet
Level	
Handsaw	
Square	
Wood chisel	
Drill with countersink bit	
2 × 6 lumber	
3½" deck screws	

For Understairs Shelves:

Work gloves	2 × 4 standard lumber
Eye protection	(for shelf supports)
Circular saw	2½" deck screws or
Level	coarse-thread wood
Drill with bits	screws
Tape measure	¾" AC (paint-grade on
2 × 4 pressure-treated	one side) plywood
lumber (for posts and	2" coarse-thread drywall
struts)	screws

How to Build Stairway Wall Shelves

1

Mark the desired height for each shelf, then use a level to transfer the mark across the front edge of each stud. Measure from your level lines to mark the location of the next shelf up or down. The lines will represent the top face of the shelves.

2

Measure along each level line and cut the 2 × 6 shelf stock to length. Hold each shelf in place on its lines and mark the side edges of each stud for the notches. *Tip: If a stud is out of square to the wall plane, make the notch big enough so the shelf will fit straight on.*

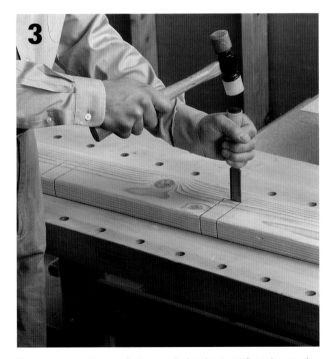

3

Use a square to mark the notch depths at 3½". Make notch marks on both sides of the shelf. Cut the sides of the notches with a handsaw. Complete the notches by chiseling straight down from both sides of the board along the seat, or base, of the notch marks.

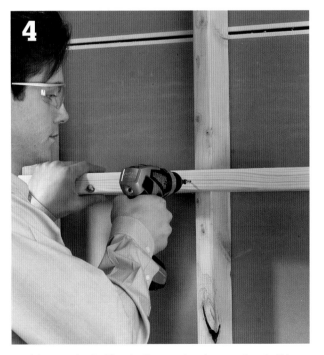

4

Position each shelf on its lines and make sure the shelf is level from front to back. Drill a pilot hole at the center of each stud location using a countersink bit. Fasten the shelf to each stud with a 3½" deck screw.

How to Build Understairs Basement Shelves

Mark the locations of the two 2 × 4 posts onto the floor. The posts must be equidistant from the bottom end of the staircase. Cut each post a little longer than needed. Position the post plumb next to the floor mark, and trace along the stair stringer to mark the angled top cut for the post.

Cut the post ends with a circular saw or power miter saw. Set each post on its floor mark and fasten the top end to the bottom edge of the stair stringer with three 2½" deck screws or wood screws driven through pilot holes.

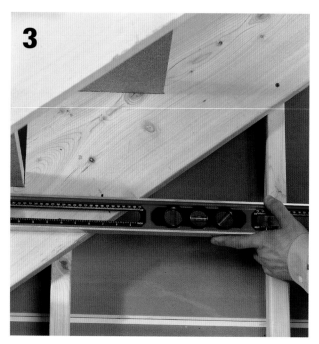

Mark the desired location of each shelf onto the stair stringers. Use a level—and a long, straight board as needed—to transfer the height marks to the inside faces of the posts.

For each shelf, measure and cut two 2 × 4 side supports to span from the outside edges of the posts to the back sides of the steps (or as far as practical). Also cut one 2 × 4 end support to span between the outside faces of the posts.

5

Fasten the side supports to the posts and stair stringers with four 2½" screws at each end. Fasten the end supports to the outside edges of the posts with two screws at each end. The end supports should be flush with the top edges of the side supports, with their ends flush with the outside faces of the posts.

Option: For long shelves that will hold heavy items, add midspan supports between the side supports. Reinforce a bottom shelf with 2 × 4 struts cut to fit between the side supports and the floor. *Note: Very heavy items should go on a reinforced bottom shelf, since stair structures aren't designed for significant extra weight loads.*

6

Cut the shelf panels to fit from ¾" plywood. The edges of the panels should be flush with the outside face of the side and end supports. Fasten the panels to the supports with 2" drywall screws.

Variation: If your staircase has a center stringer, notch the plywood shelf panels to fit around the stringer. Cut the sides of the notches with a circular saw or handsaw, and then make the seat cuts with a chisel to complete the notches.

Joist Shelves

If you think you have completely run out of storage space, but still have an unfinished ceiling somewhere in the house or garage, think again. This handy little shelf is built to fit and fold up directly between unfinished joists, storing utility items until you need them. It is a good place for tools, laundry room supplies, smaller sporting goods, or other items you don't use every day. If you plan on storing liquids on the shelf, make sure the lids are closed tightly before folding up the shelf. The design of the shelf is easy to change to make it stationary or deeper. With a minimum of effort and materials, you can build a simple storage solution for utility items.

Turn joist cavities into efficient storage cabinets with these inexpensive, easy-to-build folding shelves.

Tools, Materials & Cutting List ▸

Tools
Work gloves
Eye protection
Drill with bits
½" spade bit
Circular saw
Ratchet set
Combination square
C-clamps
Level
Tape measure

Materials
Pine lumber
 (1 × 3, 1 × 4, 1 × 6)
Pine plywood (½", ¾")
½"-dia. × 3" carriage
 bolts (2)
½" lock washers (2)
½" flat washers (4)
½" hex nuts (2)
Wood screws (#6 × 1½")
Wood glue
¼ × 2" lag screws (2)

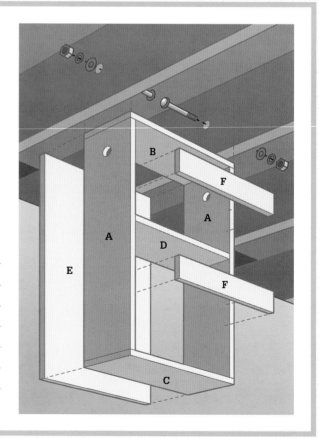

Key	Part	Dimension
A	(2) Side	¾ × 5½ × 30½" pine
B	(1) Top	¾ × 5½ × 14*" pine
C	(1) Bottom	¾ × 5½ × 14*" pine
D	(1) Middle shelf	¾ × 5½ × 12½*" pine
E	(1) Back	½ × 14* × 32" pine plywood
F	(2) Shelf rail	¾ × 2½ × 12½*" pine

*Cut to fit

How to Build Joist Shelves

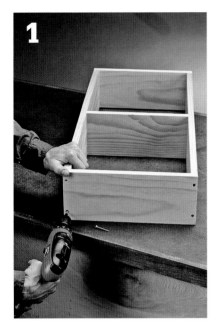

Cut the sides, shelf, top, and bottom from 1 × 6 pine and joint them together in a square frame. Make corner joints by driving countersunk wood screws through the top and bottom panels and into the ends of the sides. Apply wood glue first.

Add the rails that prevent the stored items from falling out. Also add the back panel. Then,clamp the unit between two floor joists so it is level and roughly 2" down form the subfloor above. Drill a guide hole for a pivoting carriage bolt at each side.

Thread a ½ × 3" carriage bolt through each guide hole from the unit's interior side. Secure each bolt with a washer and nut.

Attach plywood turnbuckle cleats to the joists about a foot away from the unit. The turnbuckles should be roughly 1½" wide and 2½" long. Attach each one with screws, centered on the joist. Do not overdrive the screws—you should be able to pivot the turnbuckle.

Option: For storing heavier items you can make the unit bigger, but you should secure it with a pair of lag bolts at each side so it remains stationary.

Basement Storage Wall

Storage space in a basement can be a mixed blessing. On one hand, there's usually plenty of room in a basement, and you can stash all kinds of stuff down there, out of view from your living areas. On the other hand, basements tend to be dusty, sometimes damp, and often a good home for insects and other critters, so you have to be careful what you store, especially if it's going to be there for awhile. Finished basements are more hospitable environments; however, most finishing projects leave little room for general storage, and things ends up getting crammed next to the hot water heater.

Here's a storage solution that makes any basement a great place for storage, whether the space is finished, unfinished, or something in between. In essence, this project is a floor-to-ceiling wall of simple wood cabinets with plywood doors. The doors help keep

out dust and critters, while the 2 × 4 base of the unit protects stuff on the bottom shelves from a damp floor or even minor flooding. As shown here, the cabinets are just under 24" deep, but you can make them any size you need. You can also reconfigure the shelves, doors, and cabinet dimensions to fit your space and your stuff.

How much you put into the look of the storage wall is up to you. For a nicely finished basement, you'll probably want to use cabinet-grade, hardwood-veneer plywood or medium-density fiberboard (MDF) for all of the cabinet parts and the doors. Covering the side gaps and the base and top frames with matching ¼" plywood completes the finished, built-in look. For an unfinished basement, you can simplify the project and save money by using paint-grade plywood.

The storage wall looks best when it runs from corner to corner in a basement room or alcove. But because it's anchored at top and bottom, it can also go next to a wall on only one side or be "freestanding" with open space on both sides.

Tools & Materials ▸

Tools

Work gloves
Eye protection
Chalk line
Tape measure
Plumb bob
Circular saw and straightedge guide or table saw
Level
Caulk gun
Drill with bits and drill guide (or use drill press)
Clothes iron
Sand paper
Ladder
Hammer
Clamps
Portable drill guide
Pneumatic brad nailer

Materials

2 × 4 pressure-treated lumber (for base frame)
2 × 4 standard lumber (for top frame)
16d galvanized common nails
Tapered cedar shims
Construction adhesive
Plywood (¼", ½", ¾")
Veneer edge tape (optional)
Pegboard with ¼" holes
Coarse-thread drywall screws (1¼" and 2")
2½" galvanized deck screws
1 × 2 lumber
Wood glue
1" brads
Door handles or pulls
Shelf pins
European-style (cup) hinges
Finishing materials

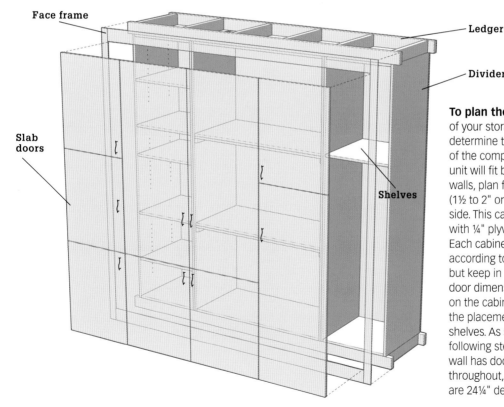

Face frame

Ledger

Divider panels

Slab doors

Shelves

To plan the dimensions of your storage wall, first determine the overall width of the completed unit. If the unit will fit between two side walls, plan for a small space (1½ to 2" or so) at either side. This can be covered with ¼" plywood trim pieces. Each cabinet can be sized according to what it will hold, but keep in mind that the door dimensions are based on the cabinet width and the placement of the fixed shelves. As shown in the following steps, the storage wall has doors of equal width throughout, and the cabinets are 24¼" deep.

How to Build a Basement Storage Wall

1

Mark the location of the base frame onto the floor. Measure out 24¼" from the back wall and make a mark at each end of the project area. Snap a chalk line between the marks. *Note: When the cabinets are installed (step 12), they will overhang the front edges of the frames by ½" and be ½" from the back wall.*

2

Use a plumb bob to transfer the chalk line location from the floor to the joists above, snap a chalk line across the joists. If the joists run parallel to the back wall, you may need to install 2 × 4 blocking between joists to support the top frame.

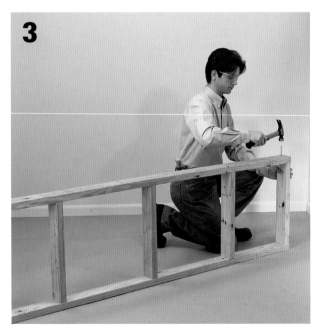

3

Build the base and top frames with 2 × 4 lumber and 16d galvanized nails, adding crosspieces spaced 24" on center. Use pressure-treated lumber for the base frame. Make the frames 23¾" wide (or ½" narrower than the cabinet depth) and their length equal to the total cabinet width.

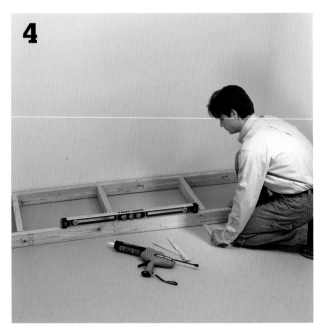

4

Install the frames with their front edges on the chalk lines. Use cedar shims as needed so the frames are perfectly level in both directions. Secure the base frame to a concrete floor with construction adhesive. Fasten the top frame to the joists with nails or screws.

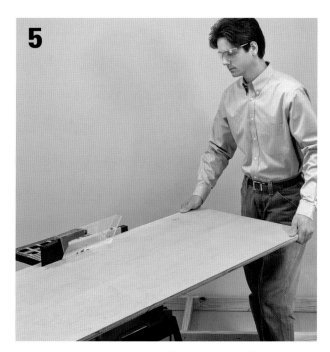

5

Measure between the top and base frames to find the cabinet height. *Tip: Leave yourself ⅛" or so of wiggle room for getting the cabinets into place.* Cut the cabinet side panels from ¾" plywood at 23¾" wide × the overall cabinet height. Use a table saw or a circular saw and edge guide to ensure straight cuts.

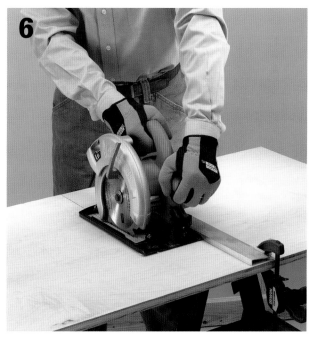

6

Cut the top and bottom cabinet panels and the fixed shelves at 23¾" deep, with the length equal to the overall cabinet width minus 1½". Cut the adjustable shelves to the same dimensions minus ⅛" in both directions. Cut the back panel from ½" plywood, equal to the overall cabinet dimensions.

7

For the cabinet(s) with adjustable shelves, drill a row of shelf-peg holes 2" from the front and back edges of the side panels using a template cut from ¼" pegboard. Make the holes ⅝" deep using a depth stop on the drill bit. Orient the template carefully so the holes are even from side to side.

8

Mark the fixed shelf locations onto the inside faces of the cabinet sides. The fixed shelves should be centered at any place where two horizontal door edges meet. Drill countersunk pilot holes through the outside faces of the side panels; the holes should meet with the centers of the top and bottom panels and the fixed shelves.

(continued)

Assemble each cabinet box with glue and 2" screws, starting with the side, top, and bottom panels and the fixed shelves. Before the glue sets up, attach the back panel with glue and 1¼" screws. Align the edges of the box with the back panel as you work to ensure the box is square.

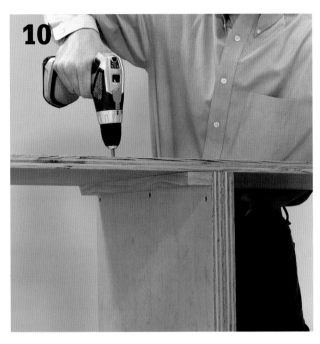

For cabinets over 30" wide, build double-layer fixed shelves with glue and 1¼" screws driven up through the bottom layer. This construction adds strength for the long span. Support the shelves with 1 × 2 cleats glued and screwed to the side and back panels. Also screw through the side and back panels into the shelf edges.

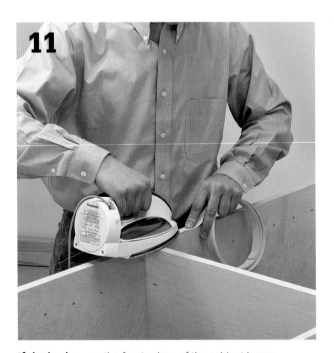

If desired, cover the front edges of the cabinet boxes with iron-on veneer edge tape that matches the plywood veneer. Slightly roundover the edges of the applied tape with sandpaper. Finish all exposed cabinet surfaces as desired, and apply at least a good seal coat to hidden surfaces to protect against moisture.

Set each cabinet in place so its front edges overhang the base and top frames by ½". Align the side edges of adjacent cabinets and fasten them together with 1¼" screws. Anchor the cabinets to the base and top frames with 2½" screws using shims to fill any gaps between the top frame and the top of the cabinets.

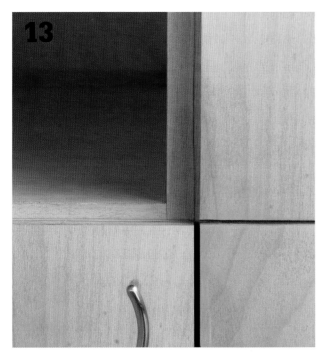

13

Cut the door panels to size from the same plywood used for the cabinet boxes. The doors should overlap the side and top/bottom cabinet panels by ⅝" and overlap any fixed shelf by ⁵⁄₁₆" (or stop ¹⁄₁₆" back from the center of doubled shelves). Apply veneer edge tape and finish the doors as desired.

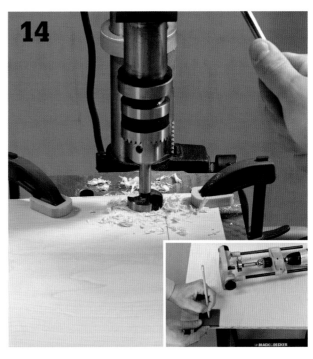

14

Drill holes for the cabinet hinges. Use a Forstner bit and drill with a drill guide (or a drill press) to make the hinge-cup holes. Follow the hinge manufacturer's specifications for hole sizes and placement. *Tip: You can buy a kit that includes the cup-hole bit and a template for marking the hinge holes (inset photo).*

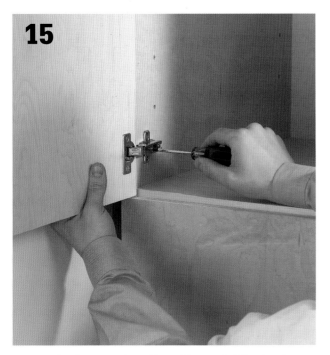

15

Mount the doors to the cabinet side panels following the manufacturer's directions. Adjust the hinges as needed so all gaps are even and the doors close properly. Install handles or pulls onto the doors. Add the adjustable shelves.

16

Option: Cut strips of ¼" veneer plywood to fit the gaps along the top, bottom, and sides of the cabinets. Install 1 × 2 or 2 × 2 backing along the sides, ½" from the cabinets' front edges. Fasten the trim to the base/top frames and the backing with 1" brads.

Utility Shelves

You can build adjustable utility shelves in a single afternoon using 2 × 4s and plain ¾" plywood. Perfect for use in a garage or basement, utility shelves can be modified by adding side panels and a face frame to create a finished look suitable for a family room or recreation area.

The quick-and-easy shelf project shown on the following pages creates two columns of shelves with a total width of 68". You can enlarge the project easily by adding more 2 × 4 risers and plywood shelves. Do not increase the individual shelf widths to more than 36". The sole plates for the utility shelves are installed perpendicular to the wall to improve access to the space under the bottom shelves.

Simple practical utility shelves are perfect for storing seasonal or large items, especially in informal spaces, such as the basement or garage.

Tools, Materials & Cutting List ▸

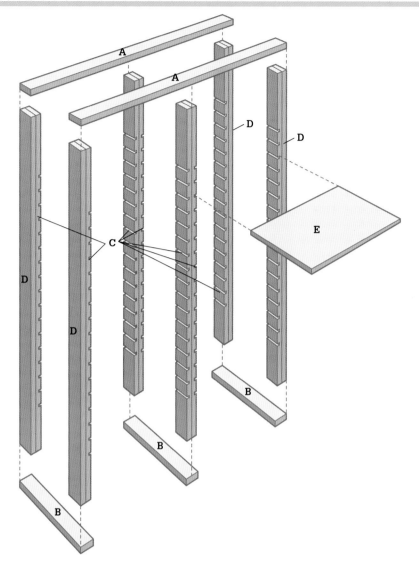

Tools

Work gloves
Eye protection
Pencil
Tape measure
Level
Framing square
Drill/driver
Plumb bob
Straightedge guide
Powder-actuated nailer
Clamps
Router with ¾" straight bit
Circular saw
Stepladder

Materials

2 × 4 pine lumber
¾" plywood
Wood glue
Shims
Drywall or deck screws
  (2½", 3")
Finishing materials

Part	No.	Desc.	Size	Material
A	2	Top plates	68"	2 × 4s
B	3	Sole plates	24"	2 × 4s
C	8	Shelf risers	93"	2 × 4s
D	4	End risers	93"	2 × 4s
E	12	Shelves	30¾ × 24"	¾" plywood

How to Build Utility Shelves

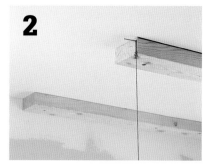

Mark the location of top plates on the ceiling. One plate should be flush against wall, and the other should be parallel to the first plate, with the front edge 24" from the wall. Cut 2 × 4 top plates to full length of utility shelves, then attach to ceiling joists or blocking using 3" screws.

Mark points directly beneath outside corners of the top plates to find outer sole plate locations using a plumb bob as a guide. Mark sole plate locations by drawing lines perpendicular to the wall connecting each pair of points.

Cut outer 2 × 4 sole plates and position them perpendicular to the wall, just inside the outlines. Shim plates to level if needed, then attach to floor with a powder-actuated nailer or 3" screws. Attach a center sole plate midway between the outer sole plates.

Prepare the shelf risers by cutting ⅞"-wide, ¾"-deep dadoes with a router. Cut dadoes every 4" along the inside face of each 2 × 4 riser, with the top and bottom dadoes cut about 12" from the ends of the 2 × 4. *Tip: Gang-cut the risers by laying them flat and clamping them together, then attaching an edge guide to align the dado cuts.* For each cut, make several passes with the router, gradually extending the bit depth until dadoes are ¾" deep.

Trim the shelf risers to uniform length before unclamping them. Use a circular saw and a straightedge guide.

Build two center shelf supports by positioning pairs of shelf risers back-to-back and joining them with wood glue and 2½" screws.

Build four end shelf supports by positioning the back of a dadoed shelf riser against a 2 × 4 of the same length, then joining the 2 × 4 and the riser with glue and 2½" screws.

Position an end shelf support at each corner of the shelving unit, between top and sole plates. Attach the supports by driving 3" screws toenail-style into the top plate and sole plates.

Position a center shelf support (both faces dadoed) at each end of the center sole plate, then anchor shelf supports to the sole plate using 3" screws driven toenail-style. Use a framing square to align the center shelf supports perpendicular to the top plates, then anchor to top plates.

Measure the distance between the facing dado grooves and subtract ¼". Cut the plywood shelves to fit and slide the shelves into the grooves.

Garage Deck

With all of its wide-open space, the garage alone could handle most long-term storage needs—that is, if you didn't also have to store your car in there (or maybe your car's already been banished to the driveway due to a serious clutter problem). As it is, garage storage is usually confined to hooks along the side walls, and perhaps a bank of shelves or cabinets in the back. But of course this isn't enough. What you need is something to take advantage of all that empty air space above the front of the car. This garage deck does just that.

The garage deck gives your vehicle all the room it needs while utilizing the wasted space above the hood. Depending on your storage needs and the ceiling height in your garage, you can make your deck low to maximize storage space, or make it high enough to walk underneath. As an example, the deck shown here is eight feet long by about five feet deep and stands four and a half feet above the floor. In a garage with a standard eight and a half feet ceiling, this deck would add about 150 cubic feet of storage space. You could double that space by building the deck so it spans all the way across a two-car garage.

In addition to the ample storage space, the best things about a garage deck are its strength and simplicity. The construction is virtually identical to an outdoor deck. It has a 2 × 6 ledger board mounted to the garage's back wall and a doubled 2 × 6 structural beam supported by 4 × 4 posts along the front. Hanging from the ledger and beam with metal framing anchors are 2 × 6 joists. Instead of a floor made of deck boards, the storage deck is covered with plywood, which is cheaper and faster to install. A 2 × 6 understructure provides plenty of strength for a deck of this size. For a larger deck, you might want to move up to 2 × 8 joists and beams. And for any size of deck, be sure to include a 4 × 4 post at least every eight feet along the beam.

A garage deck lets you park your car and store your stuff without giving up extra floor space. It also keeps stored items off the garage floor, protecting them from water damage and simplifying garage cleanup.

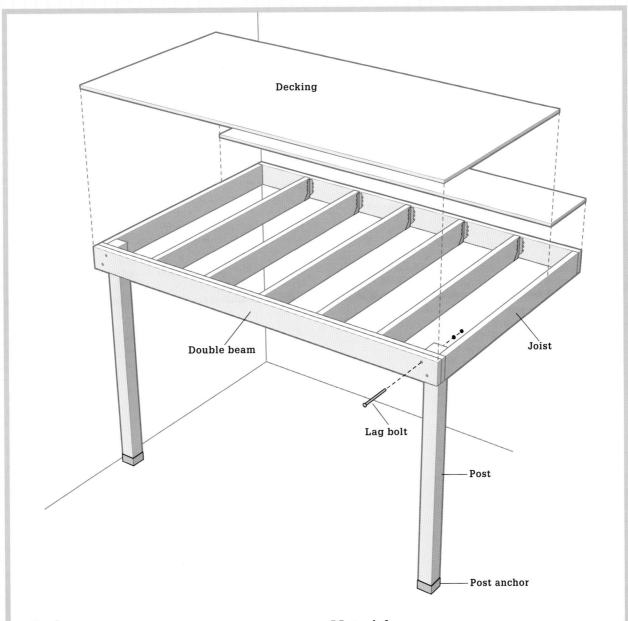

Decking

Double beam

Joist

Lag bolt

Post

Post anchor

Tools

Work gloves
Eye protection
Tape measure
Stud finder
Hammer
Level
Circular saw
Drill
Ratchet wrench

Rotary hammer
    and bit
Clamps
Chalk line
Framing square
Rafter square
Handsaw or
    reciprocating saw

Materials

2 × 6 lumber
⅜ × 5" lag screws and
    washers
Corrosion-resistant metal
    post bases
½"-dia. concrete anchors
Galvanized and standard
    common nails (10d,
    16d)
1½"-long 10d common
    nails (joist hanger nails)

8d box nails
2" deck or drywall
    screws
Construction
    adhesive
Metal joist hangers
Pressure-treated
    4 × 4 posts
½ × 8" machine bolts
    and washers
¾" plywood

How to Build a Garage Deck

Mark the height of the ledger board onto the back wall. Measure up from the floor and make a mark ¾" below the desired height of the finished deck. Use a level to draw a level line through the mark, extending the line 96" across the wall.

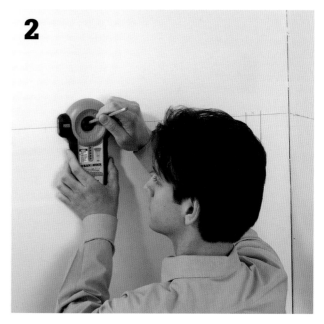

Use a stud finder to locate the studs along the back wall. Mark both side edges of each stud, just above the level line made in step 1. Extend the same level line for 6 ft. along the adjacent side wall, then mark the studs on that wall. *Note: You can also build your deck away from any side walls.*

Cut three 2 × 6s at 96" for the ledger and doubled beam. Mark the joist layout onto one of the ledger boards, spacing the joists at 16" on center. Transfer the layout to one of the remaining 2 × 6s. This will be the inside piece of the doubled beam.

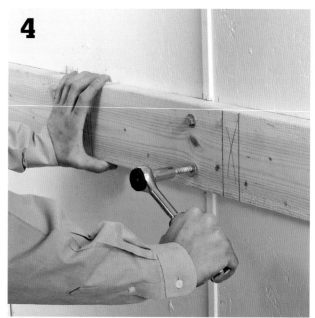

Install the ledger by first tacking it in place with a few nails, then anchoring it to each wall stud with a pair of ⅜ × 5" lag screws and washers driven through pilot holes.

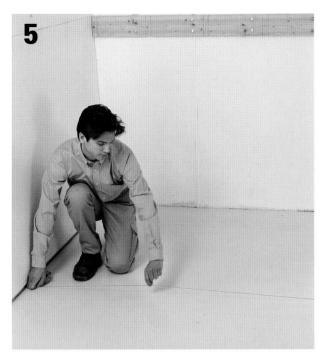

Measure out from the back wall and mark the locations of the 4 × 4 posts onto the floor. The front faces of the posts will be 3" from the front edge of the finished deck floor. Snap a chalk line between the marks, making sure the line is parallel to the back wall.

Make marks for the side-wall faces of the posts at 1½" and 91" from the side wall. At each mark, draw a reference line that's perpendicular to the chalk line made in step 5.

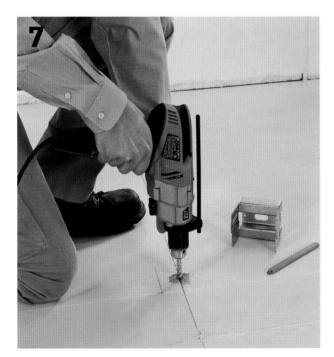

Position a post base on the perpendicular reference lines, and mark the center of the base for the anchor-bolt hole. Drill a hole for a ½"-dia. concrete anchor following the manufacturer's specifications. *Tip: A rotary hammer and bit (available for rent) is the best tool for drilling through concrete.*

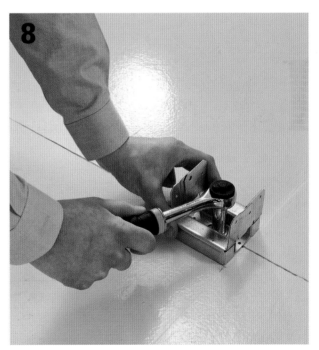

Install a ½"-dia. expansion-type or epoxy-set concrete anchor as directed by the manufacturer. Secure the post bases to the anchors with washers and nuts. Add the base platform ("standoff") to each base, if provided.

(continued)

9

Cut seven 2 × 6 joists to length, equal to the depth of the finished deck minus 4⅝" (58⅞" in project as shown). Install one joist on the side wall, flush to the level line made in step 2. Fasten the joist with pairs of 16d common nails driven into each wall stud.

10

Construct the double beam by joining the two beam boards with construction adhesive and 10d common nails driven through both sides of the beam. Make sure the boards are flush at the top, and drive the nails at a slight angle so they don't protrude from the opposite side.

11

Install metal joist hangers onto the inside faces of the beam and ledger using a scrap piece of joist material to position each hanger. Fasten the hangers with 10d common nails (or as recommended by the manufacturer).

12

Rough-cut the 4 × 4 posts a few inches longer than needed. Set each post into its base, hold it plumb, and tack it place with a few 10d galvanized common nails (or as recommended by the manufacturer).

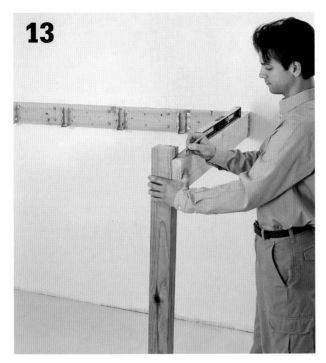

13

Nail the side-wall post to the installed end joist with 16d common nails. Install the other end joist, fastening it to the joist hanger with 1½"-long 10d common nails (or as recommended) and to the post with 16d nails. Make sure the post is plumb and the end joist is level.

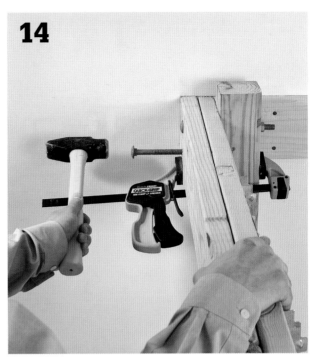

14

Clamp the beam against the outside faces of the posts, flush with the top of the end joists. Drill holes and anchor the beam to the posts with two ½ × 8" machine bolts (with washers) at each end.

15

Install the remaining joists in the hangers, making sure any bowed edges (crowning) of the boards are pointing up. Fasten the joists to the hangers with 1½"-long 10d common nails (or as recommended) using all of the holes in the hanger.

16

Trim the posts flush with the top of the end joists and beam using a handsaw or reciprocating saw. Install ¾" plywood for the decking flush with the outside edges of the deck framing. Fasten the decking with 8d box nails or 2" deck or drywall screws.

Adjustable Shelving

Some garage stuff is simply stored best on shelving, particularly if it's too large to fit into a cabinet but still relatively lightweight. Empty planters, gas cans, boxed supplies, and half-full cans of paint are ideal candidates for a sturdy shelving system. You could go to the effort and build your garage shelving from scratch, but going that route will require you to come up with a means of supporting shelf boards on the wall. It's doable, of course, but you'll have to make the standards and brackets yourself. Plus, most shop-made shelving is fixed in place, so you can't reposition the shelves easily if your storable items change.

A more convenient option is to buy metal shelf standards that fasten to the wall studs and shelf brackets that clip into a series of slots on the standards. Home centers carry these adjustable shelving systems in several colors and they come with shelf brackets in a range of lengths to suit various shelf widths. For garage applications, it's a good idea to buy heavy-duty standards and brackets. The components are made of thicker-gauge metal than regular-duty hardware, and the shelf brackets have two mounting lugs instead of one to reinforce the attachment points.

When you install your shelving, locate the tops of the standards just high enough so you can reach the top shelf from the floor. If you plan to load your shelving with fairly heavy items, mount a standard to every wall stud in the shelf area. Use strong screws recommended by the manufacturer and fasten them to wall studs only—never to paneling, trimboards, or wallboard alone. Be sure to use sturdy shelf boards and firmly tap the brackets into mounting slots before loading up the shelves.

Tools & Materials ▸

Work gloves
Eye protection
Tape measure
Level
Stud finder
Drill
Rubber mallet
Straightedge

Circular saw or
   table saw
Shelf standards and
   brackets
Installation screws
¾" plywood
Brackets

Sturdy adjustable shelves are easy to install and offer a convenient place to safely store those larger lightweight items off the floor.

How to Install Bracket Shelves

1

Install the first standard at one end of the installation area. The standards seen here (70" long) are centered on wall studs with the tops level. Align the top of the standard with the top level line and drive one screw through a mounting hole. Hold a level against the side of the standard and adjust it until it is plumb. Drive screws through the remaining mounting holes.

2

Install the remaining standards. For foolproof results, install the two end standards first and then establish a level line between them so you can butt the intermediate standards against the line. Use a level against each standard to make sure it is plumb. *Note: If you need to cut the standards for length, align all cut ends of the standards in the same locations (either at the top or the bottom).*

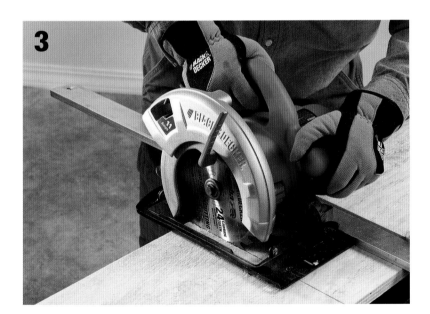

3

Prepare your shelf stock. For excellent results, rip-cut quality ¾" plywood to width (usually 11½") on a table saw or with a circular saw with a straightedge. Avoid particleboard or MDF shelving as it is prone to sagging and will degrade quickly if exposed to moisture. Most premilled shelving (usually coated with vinyl or melamine) is made from particleboard and is a bit too lightduty for garage storage. If you'd rather not rip-cut material, use utility-grade dimensional pine (1 × 12).

4

Install shelf support brackets in the standards using light blows from a rubber mallet to make sure they're fully seated. Set the shelving onto the standards, adjusting as desired.

Garage Cabinets

If you'd prefer to keep your garage storables behind closed doors, a set of cabinets might be just the solution you're looking for. Any interior kitchen cabinets can be used in a garage, including both base and upper cabinets. Base cabinets really offer several benefits: deep inner storage for large items; drawers for fasteners, hardware, or other small tools; and, of course, a convenient flat work surface. If you're upgrading your garage storage on a budget, utility-grade melamine or unfinished cabinets are actually quite affordable. You could also shop at a second-hand building materials outlet or put to use cabinets removed during a kitchen remodel. If you have limited floor space in your garage, look for utility cabinets with a shallower base. Some manufacturers offer a 15"-deep model that's 9" shallower than a standard base cabinet. As you plan, make sure there's still room to park the car, bikes, and other yard and garden equipment.

The process for installing cabinets in a garage is the same as in a kitchen. Cabinets must be firmly attached to wall studs, and they should be level and plumb. Using a level as a guide, draw reference lines along the project wall to indicate the locations of base and wall cabinets. If your garage floor is uneven, find the highest point of the floor along the wall and use this as your initial reference for drawing the other layout lines.

The best way to ensure an even, level installation of upper cabinets is to install a temporary ledger board to the wall, and rest the cabinets on it when fastening them to the wall studs. Many pros install upper cabinets first, to take advantage of the full wall access, but you might want to begin with the base cabinets and use them to help support the uppers during their installation. If your garage cabinet system will include a corner cabinet, install it first and work outward to make sure the corner cabinet will fit the space properly. If your garage floor tends to be damp, it's a good idea to install leveler feet on the base cabinets beforehand.

Tools & Materials ▸

Work gloves	Panel adhesive
Eye protection	¾" plywood
Tape measure	Lumber (1 × 2,
4 ft. level	1 × 3, 1 × 4)
Chalk line	¼"-thick hardboard
Stud finder	1" brads
Drill	Trim (optional)
Hammer	Cabinets
Shims	Leveler feet
Combination square	1¼" panhead screws
Caulk gun	2½" drywall screws
Stepladder	Filler strips
Grease pencil (or tape)	Finish nails
C-clamps	L-bracket

Garage utility cabinets are inexpensive and because the base cabinets are not as deep as kitchen cabinets, they have a compact footprint that's well suited to a garage. A durable melamine surface is easy to clean, and a double plywood work top with a replaceable hardboard surface stands up well to hard use.

How to Install Garage Cabinets

Find the high point of the floor in the installation area by leveling a long, straight board and identifying the principal contact point with the floor. Mark the point on the floor with a grease pencil or tape.

Draw a level line along the wall at the desired height to create a base cabinet top reference.

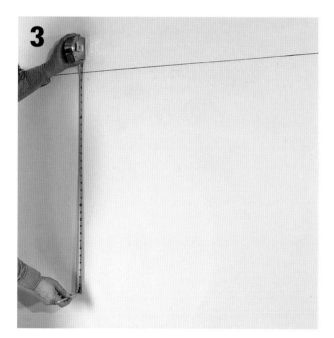

Draw reference lines for the upper cabinets based on the base cabinet line. If your base cabinets are 34½" tall (standard height not including countertop) then the line for the top of the upper cabinets should be 49½" above the base cabinet line and parallel to it. Measure down 30" from the upper cabinet top line and mark reference lines for the bottom of the upper cabinets (make sure your cabinets are 30" high first—this is a standard but there is occasional variation).

Mark wall stud locations clearly on the wall just above the base cabinets line and just below the bottom upper cabinets line. Also mark stud locations slightly above the top upper cabinet line. Use a stud finder to identify the locations of the studs.

(continued)

5

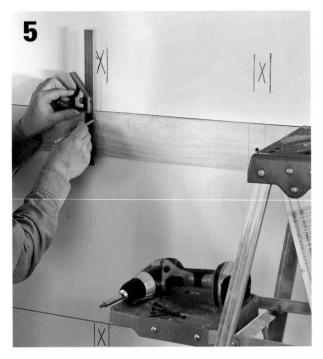

Attach ledgers to the wall or walls to provide temporary support for the upper cabinets while you install them. The ledgers (1 × 4 is being used here) should just touch the reference line for the bottom of the wall cabinet. Attach the ledger with a drywall screw driven at each stud location. Transfer stud location marks to the ledger.

6

Attach the first wall cabinet with 2½" drywall screws. If the cabinet has a mounting strip at the top of the back panel (most do), drive a pair of screws through the strip at each stud location. Attach all wall cabinets to the wall.

7

Join wall cabinets by driving 1¼" panhead screws through one cabinet side and into the adjoining cabinet side. Clamp the cabinets together first to make sure the fronts and tops stay flush.

8

Install the first base cabinet directly under the first wall cabinet. Position the cabinet and shim it as needed until it is level, plumb, and touches the reference line (see step 2). Secure it to the wall with 2½" drywall screws.

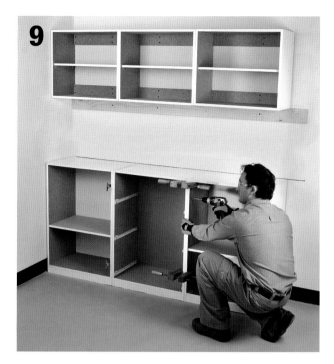

9

Install the remaining base cabinets by leveling, screwing to the wall studs, and then fastening the cabinet sides together. Attach toekick trim boards or side panel trim, if desired. Remove the upper cabinet wall ledger or ledgers.

10

Attach cabinet doors and drawers if you removed them during installation or if they were not preattached. Adjust the hinges according to the manufacturer's instructions so the gaps between doors are even and they all open and close smoothly.

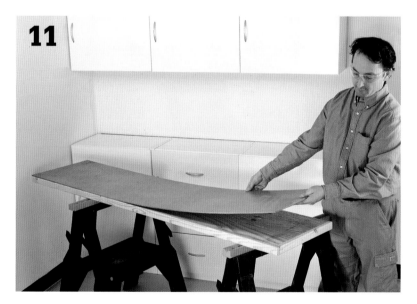

11

Make the work top. While a piece of postform countertop makes a suitable and easy to install work top, you can create a heavier, more durable top with plywood. Simply cut two pieces of ¾" plywood so they overhang each side and the front of the cabinet base by 1". Secure them with panel adhesive and countersunk 1¼" screws. Use plenty of screws. Then cover the front and side edges with strips of 1 × 2s. The front strip should overhang the front ends of the side strips. Attach the strips with adhesive and finish nails. Finally, cut a piece of ¼"-thick hardboard so all edges are flush with the base. Attach it with 1" brads driven through slightly countersunk pilot holes (the heads need to be recessed). When the hardboard top becomes worn, you can easily remove it and replace it.

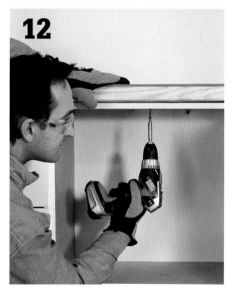

12

Attach the work top. If your base cabinets do not have preattached mounting strips for a countertop, fasten L-brackets around the inside perimeter of each cabinet and then drive screws up through the L-brackets and into the underside of the work top. Apply a bead of panel adhesive to all cabinet top surfaces for a better bond and to reduce clattering. Add a bench vise, if desired.

Garage Ceiling Storage

Some garage storables, such as empty coolers, luggage, and cartop carriers, tend to be bulky but lightweight. They take up an inordinate amount of shelf or floor space that could be better used for heavier items. One storage option for these items is right above your head—on your garage ceiling. Aside from a few lights and the track rails for your garage door, there isn't much on the ceiling of most garages. If your garage has roof trusses, you've got the perfect location for some lightweight shelf storage.

There are several ceiling-hung shelf kits available in a range of lengths and widths. The typical ceiling storage unit consists of four downrods that bolt to the bottom truss or joist members. A pair of crossbraces attaches to the downrods to form support frameworks for wire shelf grids. Other styles of ceiling storage are available for hoisting bicycles, truck toppers, or canoes up and out of the way.

Installing ceiling storage involves locating truss chords, joists, or rafter ties to support the four downrods, and then attaching the rods to the ceiling framing with lag bolts. The crossbraces and grids fit between the downrods and attach with nuts and bolts.

It's possible to install the system by yourself, but a helper makes the job much easier. Once the parts are assembled, carefully double-check all connections before loading up the shelf.

Be careful to position your ceiling storage unit clear of the path of your sectional garage door and the moving parts of your garage door opener. Use a stud finder to help determine the thickness of the trusses so you can locate the attachment bolts as close as possible to their centers. Refer to the instructions that come with your kit to be clear about the maximum weight load your unit can hold.

Tools & Materials ▸

Work gloves	Drill
Eye protection	Sockets and
Stepladder	ratchet
Stud finder	Bolts and nuts
Tape measure	Shelving and supports

A ceiling shelf unit takes advantage of underused space between the hood of your parked car and the ceiling. Most units are rated only for relatively light storage items.

How to Install a Ceiling Storage Unit

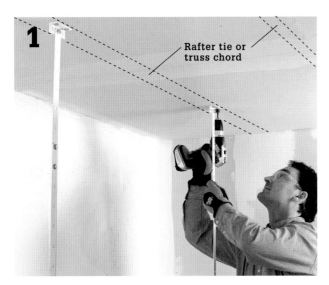

1

Rafter tie or truss chord

Attach the downrods for the first pair of horizontal support bars using the fasteners recommended by the manufacturer. The fasteners must be driven into structural members in the ceiling, be they truss chords, rafter ties, or ceiling joists. The outside edges of the two foot plates should follow the spacing recommended in the instructions (69" apart for the model seen here). Install the second pair of downrod foot plates on the next rafter or truss chord in 24" on-center framing. If the ceiling is 16" on center, skip one member so the foot plates are 32" apart.

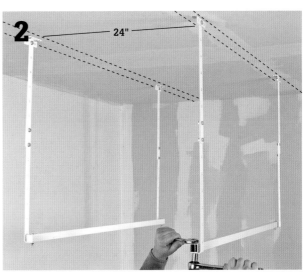

2

24"

Install the horizontal support bars. The bottom end of the downrods are secured to the horizontal bars that support the shelving. This is often done with the use of L-shaped corner rods with female ends that accept the male ends of the downrod and the horizontal bars. How deeply the corner rods are inserted into the downrod determines the height of the storage platform. Set the height you want and then insert bolts through the aligned bolt holes in the downrods and corner rods. Align all parts and secure with bolts and nuts.

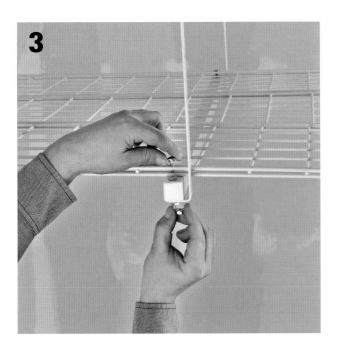

3

Install the shelving grids. Position the wire grid shelves so they span the support bars with even overhang (if possible). Thread bolts through the parallel wires and support framework as directed. Hand-tighten nuts and washers onto bolts.

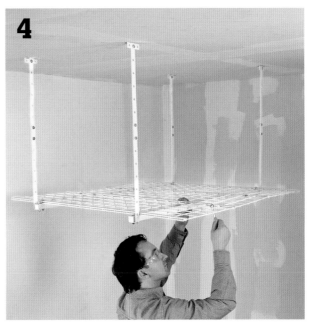

4

Join the grids together with the supplied fasteners. Load the storage items onto the shelves. Do not overload. Your instruction manual will inform you of the weight capacity. The model shown here is rated for up to 300 pounds provided the weight is distributed evenly.

Attic Storage Deck

An unfinished attic space can be a great location for long-term storage, especially for bulky, lightweight items like boxes of holiday decorations. However, unless your house was built with decking over the framing in the attic, there's no good place to set things down without risk of them falling between the joists and through the ceiling surface below. And doing the "ladder walk" across the tops of the joists to load and unload boxes is always a bad idea.

Until recently, the conventional way to add storage decking in the attic was to lay down sheets of plywood, but this comes with a few drawbacks. First, you have to cut the sheets into manageable pieces that can fit through the attic scuttle. Plywood also adds unnecessary weight to a structure that's typically not designed for heavy loads (see caution at right). Finally, plywood hides from view any electrical cables and plumbing lines running through the joists.

Plastic decking panels, like the ones shown in this project, provide the same stable surface as plywood without all the drawbacks. The small lightweight panels are made to fit over standard 16" or 24" on-center joist framing, and their open-grid structure provides visibility to utility lines below. Each panel fastens directly to the joists with screws. The panels' edges interlock with one another to create a continuous deck surface. You can also use individual panels to create a walkway for safely accessing the main storage surface.

A few words of caution for planning your storage deck: the structural framing that makes up an attic "floor" surface is primarily designed to support the ceiling surface below and may not be sufficient for heavy loads imposed by stored items. This applies to both traditional (rafter) framing and truss framing. If you have a lot of heavy items to store, it's a good idea to have the attic structure inspected by a qualified building professional to assess its safe load-bearing capacity. Any change in the ceiling surface below an attic storage deck—such as sagging, popped fasteners, or cracks in the ceiling finish—may indicate that the framing is overloaded. Also be aware that unfinished attics tend to be very hot in summer and very cold in winter, so make sure the items you store up there can handle the temperature extremes.

Tools & Materials ▸

Work gloves
Eye protection
Particle mask
Tape measure
Plastic decking panel

Manufacturer screws
Drill
Pilot bit

Unlike plywood, plastic decking panels easily fit into a car's trunk and are a breeze to haul up to an attic. For improved access to your new storage deck, consider installing a pull-down access ladder (see page 201).

Plan the decking installation by measuring the available space and determining the desired size of the deck. Inspect the area carefully for wiring and plumbing runs; never place a panel directly over wires or pipes. Measure the joist spacing, then calculate the number of panels needed to create the deck, plus any needed for access walkways. *Note: If the insulation in the joist cavities is taller than the joists, replace the insulation in the decking area with thinner insulation of the same R-value or add nailers to the tops of the joists. Compressing the existing insulation will decrease its effectiveness.*

Attic Walkways ▸

You can create a walkway using continuous rows of panels (left) or stagger the panels in stepping stone fashion (right). Include at least one panel per joist space when the walkway is perpendicular to the joists. Install additional panels around the access opening to create a comfortable "landing" area.

How to Install an Attic Storage Deck

To begin the decking installation, set the first panel in place so the side tabs are centered over the two joists.

Fasten the panel in place with the provided screws, driving the screws through the predrilled holes in the panel tabs and into the joists.

Set the next panel in place, snug against the first, and fasten it with screws. Install the remaining panels in the first row, making sure the tabs are centered over the joists.

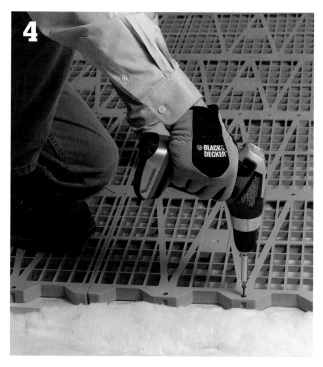

Install the panels in the next row, locking the side tabs with those of the first-row panels. Install the remaining panels following the same process.

Installing an Attic Access Ladder ▸

Now that you've added a deck to create a handy storage space in your attic, you might want to install a retractable ladder for quick and easy access. A basic wooden ladder is suitable for occasional use, while an aluminum model may offer better stability for frequent access. Measure the ceiling height below the attic access opening, as well as the joist spacing, and choose a ladder with compatible dimensions. The following is an overview of the basic installation; be sure to follow the manufacturer's instructions that come with your ladder. You might be able to use your existing access opening, or you can create a new one, as shown here.

If you plan to access your attic storage frequently, or if you plan to store heavy items up there, always have your attic inspected by a professional before beginning construction.

Mark the dimensions of the opening (as directed) onto the attic joists. If the opening is larger than a joist cavity, you'll need to cut out the center joist. Build temporary supports in the room below to support each end of the cut joist. Cut the joist, then install header pieces to support the cut ends. Add a side piece of joist lumber between the headers to frame the side of the opening.

Cut out the ceiling drywall along the edges of the framed opening, and fasten the surrounding drywall to all sides of the frame. Position the ladder unit in the opening (some come with support clips; others require temporary support boards). Anchor the ladder unit to the frame as directed.

Extend the ladder, keeping the final section folded back. Measure the required distance for the final section, then cut it to length as directed. Add adjustable feet to the end of the final section (if applicable). Install molding around the access opening, leaving adequate space for smooth operation of the ladder door panel.

Workshops

If you're stopping at this chapter, chances are you're thinking about squeezing a workshop into your garage, basement, or utility room, or you already have an integrated shop and it's starting to burst at the seams. Rest assured you're not alone. Most home hobbyists fight an ongoing battle with space constraints, and general storage is always one of the biggest (if not the biggest) challenges. The problem is that workshops, like kitchens, have to contain not only the tools and materials for work, but also the open spaces and surfaces for getting the work done. You simply can't have an efficient operation if your tools are in one location and your bench or craft table are somewhere else.

Often, the answer lies in creative problem solving. For example, simple solutions such as rolling carts for heavy equipment and pop-up work surfaces can speed the transition from garage to workshop. As for cleanup, your best bet is to get into the habit of managing the mess as you go. Small shops just don't have the space to support large scrap piles without tripping you up.

In this chapter:

- Storage Strategies
- Carousel Shelf
- Fold-down Work Shelf
- Pegboard
- Slat Wall

Storage Strategies

Whether your workshop is geared toward furniture making or scrapbooking, your stored tools and supplies should be well organized, easy to access, and out of the way. This is the best way to ensure your work surfaces are clean and ready for the next phase of a project. Depending on the type of work you do, you'll probably need plenty of open space to facilitate large projects as needed, or to temporarily reconfigure the shop to accommodate materials that need to be cut down to a manageable size, etc. If this requires the use of shared spaces—for example, making room in the garage by pulling the car into the driveway—it helps to have tools and work surfaces that are easily moved or can be set up and knocked down quickly.

Here are some of the key strategies that help make an integrated shop work with its surroundings:

For storage, think volume, not just floor space. Shelving units that rise from floor to ceiling make better use of floor space than shelves that stop at a convenient, reachable height. The upper shelves can be filled with seldom-used items. Also look for opportunities where overhead storage can help keep the floor area and work surfaces clear. Open stud cavities in an unfinished garage or utility room offer free space for small shelves or long, thin material stored on end.

For work that involves multiple stages or tool operations, plan for mobility and adaptability. Work benches, materials racks, and even large stationary tools can be outfitted with heavy-duty locking casters so you can roll them out when you need them and roll them back when you're done. You can build your own caster bases or shop around for compatible manufactured versions. Some power tools are designed for use with specific portable bases or come with their own folding stands, so check with the manufacturers of your tools.

A utility shop. This compact shop area was made with inexpensive utility cabinets and a plywood work top.

You can build this space-saving lumber rack with a few
2 × 4 studs and some steel pipe: drill matching holes in all of
the studs, then fasten one to the side of every other garage-
wall stud. Add a plywood shelf or two for storing small pieces.
*Note: Don't use garage wall studs as the pipe supports; the
holes would weaken the studs too much.*

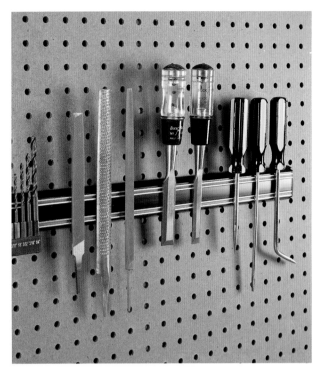

Magnetic bar strips, typically used for holding knives in the
kitchen, are just as handy for storing chisels, files, awls, and
other metal tools in the workshop.

Plan workstations for double duty: a permanent
bench or work table is already taking up floor
space, so why not use the space above and below
for storage? For example, a lumber rack above a
saw table makes it easy to grab stock as you go.
Rolling carts or pull-out bins and drawers beneath
a bench can hold other tools plus blades or bits for
the station's main tool. Small woodworking shops
can save space by combining a table saw table or
extension wing with a router table.

Consider using outdoor spaces for work and
storage. Rolling tool bases and portable workstations
simplify setup outdoors. Cutting sheet goods
(especially MDF and particleboard) outdoors helps
keep dust down in garage shops and simplifies
transport of materials into basement workspaces. A
simple lean-to shed built against the back wall of the
house or garage is a great way to keep materials out of
the elements and out of the way. A permanent outdoor
workbench made with weather-resistant materials is
handy for rough-cutting materials or finishing projects
in nice weather. Here are some other tips for saving
space in a small shop:

- Cover garage or basement walls with plywood for
  hanging tools, bins, or cabinets wherever you need
  them. Paint the plywood a light color for better
  light reflection.
- Store lumber, sheet goods, and other large materials
  on a rolling cart or rack for easy access and to
  facilitate unloading and transport from your vehicle.
- Build custom cubbies or shelving for storing
  frequently used equipment, like portable power
  tools, without their bulky cases. Incorporate tote-
  away boxes or sliding trays for blades, bits, and
  accessories.
- Keep a trash barrel or bin underneath one or both
  ends of workstations for discarding scrap material
  as you work.
- In a basement shop, store clamps and similar
  devices by clamping them to the floor joists above
  (secure bar clamps to only one joist; clamping
  across joists can pull them together, thus releasing
  other clamps)
- For a lightweight, portable work table, use a
  hollow-core door finished with polyurethane (or
  other varnish) laid over foldup metal sawhorses.

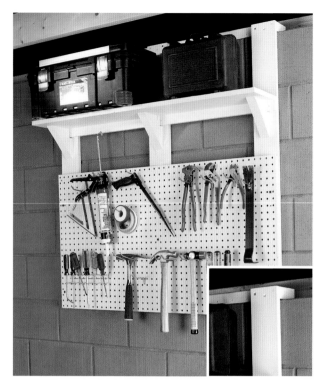

Custom hanging shelves like these provide storage in a basement workshop or craft space without the need to anchor into concrete foundation walls. The cleat along the top hooks onto the edge of a wall (inset) and can be screwed into the wood mud sill, if necessary.

Lengths of plastic plumbing pipe or cardboard carpet-roll tubes make a safe and handy home for dowels, rods, and fine trim pieces. Gang the cylinders together with strapping or duct tape to create a freestanding storage unit.

For the Handyperson ▸

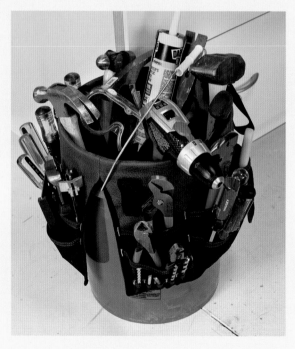

If you're the type who works on shop projects as well as DIY home repairs, you know that a lot of the same tools get used for both. You also know that grabbing a handful of tools from your shop for each home fix-it job inevitably results in multiple trips back for one more tool. The solution? Store your favorite go-to (general purpose) tools in a canvas bag or a bucket fitted with a pocket organizer. Keep the bag at your workbench so the tools are always there for projects and you can easily haul the lot of them into the house on the next repair call.

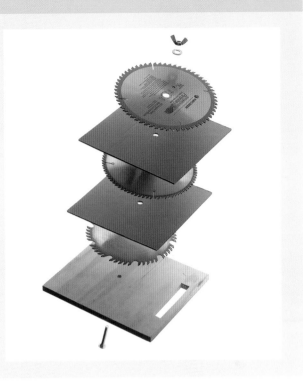

Use a plywood scrap to make a convenient caddy for storing saw blades and carrying them to a job site. Use a jigsaw to cut a carrying handle in the top of the plywood. Drill a ⅜" hole through the center of the plywood, and secure the blades with a 3" carriage bolt, wing nut, and washer. Place cardboard between the blades to protect the teeth from damage.

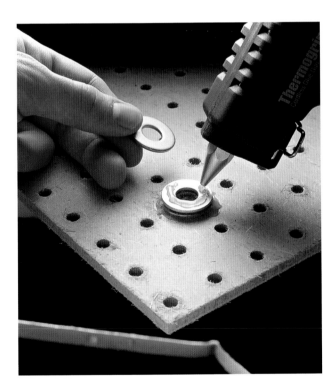

Create pegboard storage panels for stud walls. Instead of using furring strips, hot-glue pairs of washers to the back of the pegboard as spacers, so that pegboard hooks can be inserted. Hang the pegboard panel by anchoring it to every other wall stud using 2" wallboard screws.

Use plastic bottles for workshop storage. Keep clean rags handy for painting and finishing projects by storing them in plastic containers hung from a pegboard storage panel. Rags soaked in mineral spirits or other solvent-based liquids pose a fire hazard. Let dirty rags dry outdoors, then throw them away with household trash.

Storing saw accessories with ease. Attach pegboard to the sides of a table saw stand to create storage space for spare saw blades, adjustment wrenches, and other table saw accessories. Attach the pegboard by drilling holes in the legs of the saw stand and mounting the pegboard panel with machine screws and nuts.

Build a Bench Buddy. Create more storage space by attaching pieces of pegboard to the sides of the workbench with wallboard screws and finish washers.

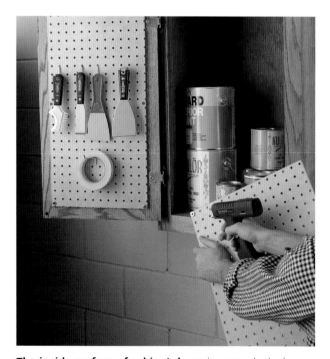

The inside surface of cabinet doors is an overlooked storage area. To make use of this space, attach small pegboard panels with ½" wallboard screws. Glue pairs of metal washers on the back of the pegboard as spacers to provide room for pegboard hooks to be inserted.

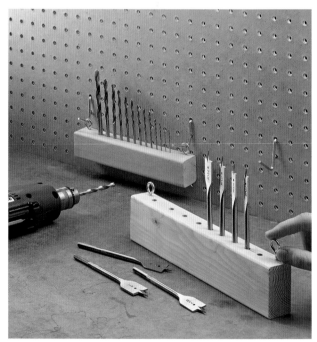

Metal drill and router bits have finely honed cutting edges that can be ruined if the bits bump against each other inside a toolbox or workbench drawer. To protect tool bits from damage, make a storage block by boring holes in a scrap piece of lumber. Attach screw eyes to the top of the block so it can be stored on pegboard hooks and taken down when a bit is needed.

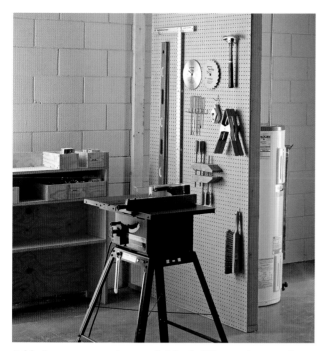

Add storage space in an unfinished utility area by covering the studs with panels of pegboard. These panels are ideal for storing wallboard framing squares, levels, garden tools, and other large items.

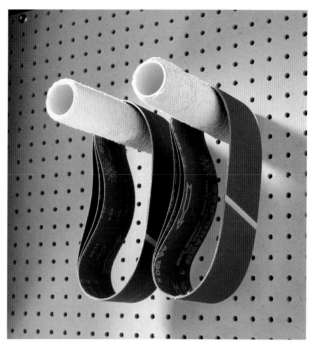

Sanding belt storage. Sanding belts stored in a drawer or toolbox can get creased or flattened and lose their effectiveness. To avoid this, hang sanding belts from old paint roller covers or pieces of PVC plumbing pipe attached to pegboard hooks.

Pegboard hooks frequently fall out when an item is removed. End this aggravating problem by gluing the hooks to the pegboard with a hot glue gun. If you need to reposition the pegboard hooks, heat them for a few seconds with a heat gun until the glue softens.

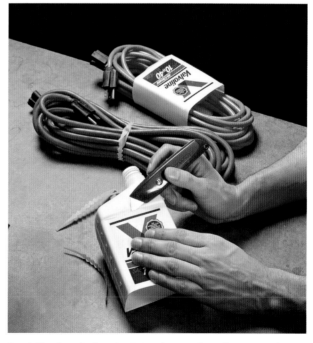

Beat the tangle tussle. Extension cords and power tool cords often become knotted and tangled. To keep a cord neatly coiled, cut off the ends of a clean plastic motor oil bottle and slip it over the coiled electrical cord. Or secure cords with the ties from plastic garbage bags.

The inside wall above a garage door makes a good storage space. Use this area to store long pieces of wood molding, dimension lumber, or plumbing pipe. Attach metal or wooden support brackets to the sleeper studs or header. Metal brackets available at any hardware store or home center can be attached to the front of sleeper studs with long wallboard screws or lag screws. Or cut L-shaped wooden brackets from scrap plywood and attach them to the sides of the sleeper studs with 2" wallboard screws. To provide adequate support, space the brackets no more than 36" apart.

Store long materials in the space between open ceiling joists in an unfinished utility area. Attach ¾" plywood furring strips across the joists with 2½" wallboard screws or lag screws. Space the strips no more than 36" apart to provide adequate support. Make sure to avoid any electrical cables or fixtures located between the ceiling joists. Some homeowners attach boards across the bottom of the ceiling joists to make out-of-the-way storage shelves for small cans and other shop items.

Use leftover pieces of plywood or 1" lumber to build sturdy storage boxes for heavy hardware. Assemble the boxes with 1¼" wallboard screws. Organize the storage boxes on utility shelves for easy access. If you wish, attach metal handles to the boxes. Wooden drawers from a discarded desk or dresser also make good storage boxes.

Hang 'em high. Use large rubber-coated lag hooks to store power tools off the floor and away from dirt and moisture. Anchor the lag hooks securely to ceiling joists or cross blocking.

Keep extension cords tangle free by storing them in 5-gal. plastic buckets. Cut a hole in the side of the bucket near the bottom. Thread the pronged extension cord plug through the hole from the inside, then coil the cord into the bucket. The extension cord will remain tangle free when pulled from the bucket. You can also use the bucket to carry tools to a work site.

Protect and organize expensive router bits by lining a workbench drawer with rigid foam or foam rubber. Cut out recesses in the foam so the finely honed cutting edges do not bump against other objects.

How to Coil Extension Cords ▶

1. Hold the end of the extension cord in one hand. Use the other hand to loop the extension cord back and forth in a figure-eight pattern until it is completely coiled.
2. Take one of the cord loops and wrap it twice around one end of the coil.
3. Insert the loop trough the center of the coil, and pull it tight. Store the cord by hanging it from this loop.

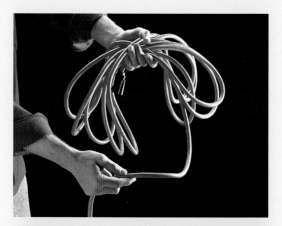

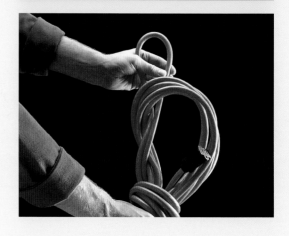

Organize a collection of pipe clamps and bar clamps by storing them on a 2 × 4 attached to wall studs. Anchor the 2 × 4 to the studs with 3" wallboard screws or lag screws.

Carousel Shelf

A carousel shelf improves access to cramped areas, like the space underneath a stairway. The turntable bearing used for this project is available at woodworking stores.

Tools & Materials ▸

Work gloves
Eye protection
Pencil
Drill
Bits (⅜" masonry,
  ¾" spade)
Hammer
Screwdriver
12" turntable
  bearing

Plastic masonry
  anchors
¾" plywood disk
  (3 ft. dia.)
¾" wallboard screw
#8 1½" sheet metal
  screws

How to Install a Carousel Shelf on a Concrete Floor

1

Position the turntable bearing on the floor. Locate the holes for masonry anchors by rotating the bearing and marking the floor through the large access opening in the top of the bearing.

2

Remove the turntable bearing and drill 2"-deep anchor holes at the marked points using a ⅜" masonry bit. Insert the masonry anchors into the floor holes.

3

Position the bearing upside down on the plywood disk., making sure it is centered. Mark the location of the large access opening on the disk. Remove the bearing and drill a ¾" access hole in the disk. Reposition the bearing and attach it to the disk with ¾" wallboard screws.

4

Position the carousel on the floor. Rotate the plywood disk and drive 1½" sheet metal screws into the floor anchors through the access opening.

Fold-down Work Shelf

The plan is for a 24 × 30" workshelf attached to masonry walls, but the design can be changed to meet your workshop needs. For clearance, the shelf width should be ½" less than the space between the framing members. If desired, install pegboard storage panels between the framing members.

 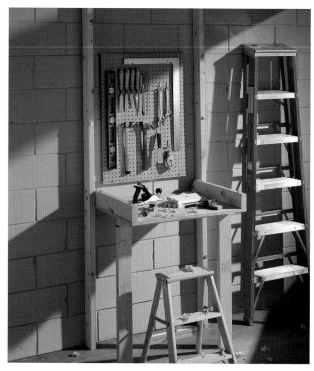

Make the most of limited workshop space by building a fold-down work shelf. The work shelf can be mounted from exposed wall studs, or from a frame attached to masonry walls. When it is not in use, fold the work shelf up and out of the way.

Tools, Materials & Cutting List ▶

Tools
Work gloves
Eye protection
Tape measure
Pencil
Saw
Drill
Drill bits (⅜" spade,
⅝" masonry, ⅛" twist)
Level
Hammer
Caulk gun
Ratchet wrench
Screwdriver
Combination square

Materials
2 × 4 lumber
⅝" masonry anchors (4)
Panel adhesive
⅜ × 6" lag screws with
washers (4)
¾" plywood (24 × 30")
⅜ × 5" carriage bolts with
washers and nuts (4)
2" wallboard screws
3" hinges (2)
⅜ × 4" bolts with washers
and nuts (2)
⅜" dowel (3" long)

Key	Part	Dimension
A	2	2 × 4 work shelf framing members, 6 ft. long
B	2	2 × 4 work shelf sides, 24" long, cut as shown
C	1	¾" plywood shelf, 24 × 30"
D	1	2 × 4 shelf support, 30" long
E	2	2 × 4 legs, 32" long

How to Build a Fold-down Workshelf

Set the framing members (A) on edge and drill two holes down through each piece using a ⅜" spade bit. Position one of the holes 18" from the end of the 2 × 4, and position the other hole 36" from the first hole.

Position framing members against the wall, and mark hole locations for the masonry anchors using a pencil. Framing members should be spaced 32" apart (on center) and must be plumb. Drill 2"-deep holes in the wall using a ⅝" masonry bit.

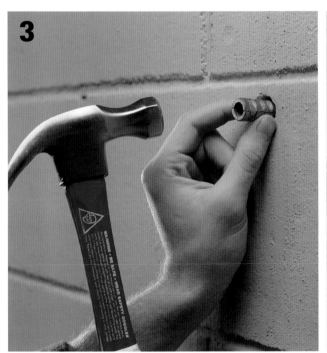

Tap a ⅝" masonry anchor into each hole. Apply a thick bead of panel adhesive to the back of each framing member. Anchor the framing members to the walls with ⅜ × 6" lag screws and washers using a ratchet wrench.

(continued)

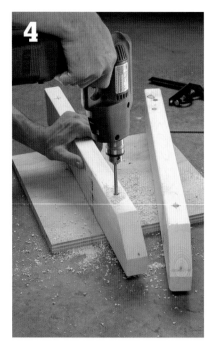

Position the work shelf sides on edge and drill two ⅜" holes down through each piece. Position one hole 4½" from the angled end of the 2 × 4, and position the other hole 2½" from the square end.

Lay the work shelf sides flat. On each piece, mark a point 1½" from the angled end of the 2 × 4 and 1½" from the bottom edge. Drill a ⅜" hole at each point.

Position the work shelf sides on the plywood shelf, with the edges flush and the square ends facing the same direction. Use a pencil to mark hole locations on the plywood. Remove the sides, and drill ⅜" holes through the plywood.

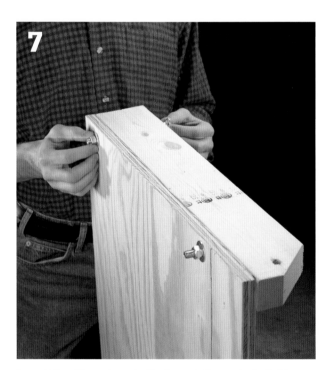

Insert ⅜ × 5" carriage bolts through the work shelf sides and the plywood shelf. Join the pieces together with washers and nuts, and tighten with a ratchet wrench.

Set the work shelf upside down. Position the shelf support on the bottom of the work shelf, about 5" from the front edge. Attach the shelf support with 2" wallboard screws driven every 8".

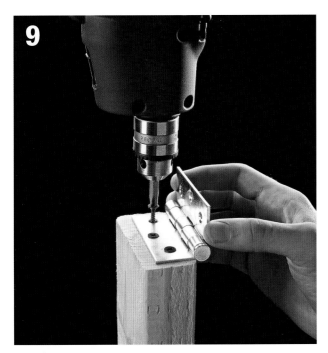

9

Attach a 3" hinge to the end of each leg using 2" wallboard screws. The edge of the leg should be flush with the edge of the hinge pin. Drill ⅛" pilot holes to prevent screws from splitting the wood at the end grain.

10

Attach the legs to the work shelf by screwing the hinges to the shelf support with 2" wallboard screws. The hinge pins should just touch the back edge of the shelf support.

11

Drill a ⅜" mounting hole in the center of each framing member, 36" above the floor.

12

Position the work shelf between the framing members and attach it with ⅜ × 4" bolts, washers, and nuts. Tighten the nuts with a ratchet wrench until snug.

13

Raise the work shelf to the upright (closed) position. Make a shelf lock by drilling a ⅜" hole through one of the framing members and partway into the side of the shelf. Insert a 3" length of ⅜" dowel to keep the work shelf in the upright position when not in use.

Pegboard

Pegboard, also called perforated hardboard or perfboard, is one of the simplest and least expensive storage solutions for hanging tools and other lightweight objects. When mounted to the wall and outfitted with metal hooks, pegboard provides a convenient way to keep items from getting lost in the back of a drawer or the bottom of a tool chest. Pegboard also makes it easy to change the arrangement or collection of your wall-hung items, because you can reposition the metal hooks any way you like without measuring, drilling holes, or hammering nails into the wall. In fact, pegboard has served as a low-cost storage option for so long that there are a multitude of different hooks and brackets you can buy to accommodate nearly anything you want to hang. Any home center will carry both the pegboard and the hooks.

You need to install pegboard correctly to get the most value from it. If your garage walls have exposed studs, you can simply screw pegboard to the studs. The empty bays between the studs will provide the necessary clearance for inserting the hooks. On a finished wall, however, you'll need to install a framework of furring strips behind the pegboard to create the necessary clearance and provide some added stiffness. It's also a good idea to build a frame around your pegboard to give the project a neat, finished appearance.

If your garage tends to be damp, seal both faces of the pegboard with several coats of varnish or primer and exterior paint; otherwise it will absorb moisture and swell up or even delaminate.

Tools & Materials ▸

Work gloves	Caulk gun
Eye protection	Drywall screws (1", 2½")
Tape measure	Panel adhesive
Level	Picture frame molding
Circular saw or jigsaw	(optional)
Drill with bits	Paint roller
Stud finder	Varnish or primer and
Clamps	paint
1 × 2" furring strips	Pegboard

Pegboard systems are classic storage solutions for garages and other utility areas. Outfitted with a variety of hangers, they offer flexibility and convenience when used to store hand tools and other small shop items.

Pegboard & Hanger Hardware Styles ▸

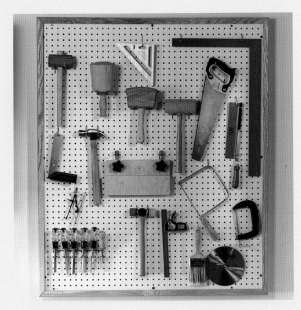

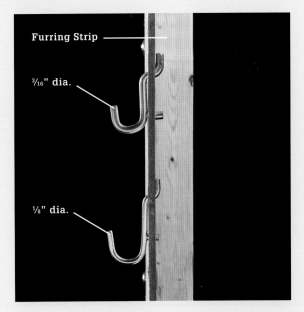

Hanger hardware comes in many shapes and sizes, from the basic J for hanging a single tool to double-prong hangers for hammers and even shelf standards. You can buy assorted hangers in kits or stock up on the type you're likely to use the most.

Two common thicknesses for pegboard hangers are ⅛"-dia. and ³⁄₁₆"-dia., both of which fit into standard pegboard hole configurations. The thicker the hanger, the more it can handle. Both types rely on the mechanical connection with the pegboard and can fail if the holes in the board become elongated. The pegboard must have furring strips on the back side to create a recess for the hangers.

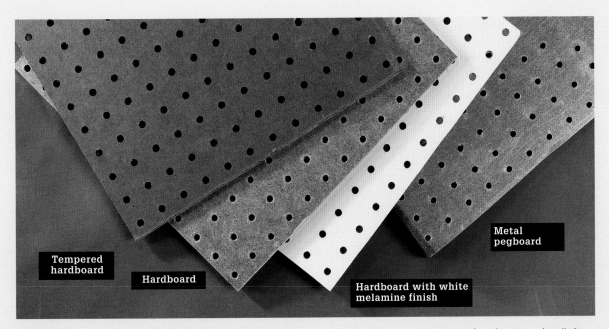

Pegboard is a single-purpose sheet good material. It is used to create a wall surface with storage function (occasionally it may be used as a cabinet back where ventilation is desired). Although it comes in ⅛"-thick panels, avoid them in favor of ¼" thick material. Most larger home centers carry it unfinished and in prefinished white. Wood grain and other decorative panels can be found, and you can also buy metal pegboard panels. The standard size holes are ¼" dia. and spaced in a 1" on center grid.

How to Install a Pegboard Storage System

Cut your pegboard panel to size if you are not installing a full sheet (most building centers sell 2 × 4 ft. and 4 × 4 ft. panels in addition to the standard 4 × 8 ft.) If you are cutting with a circular saw, orient the panel face up to prevent tearout on the higher-grade face. If cutting with a jigsaw, the good face of the panel should be down. If possible, plan your cuts so there is an even amount of distance from the holes to all edges.

Cut 1 × 2 furring strips to make a frame that is attached to the back side of the pegboard panel. The outside edges of the furring strips should be flush with the edges of the pegboard. Because they will be visible, cut the frame parts so the two side edge strips run the full height of the panel (36" here). Cut a couple of filler strips to fill in between the top and bottom rails.

Attach the furring strips to the back of the panel using 1" drywall screws and panel adhesive. Drive the screws through countersunk pilot holes in the panel face. Do not drive screws through the predrilled pegboard holes. Use intermediate furring strips to fill in between the top and bottom. These may be fastened with panel adhesive alone.

Option: Make a frame from picture frame molding and wrap it around the pegboard to conceal the edge grain and the furring strips. If you can't find picture frame molding with the correct dimensions, mill your own molding by cutting a ⅜"-wide by 1"-deep rabbet into one face of 1 × 2 stock.

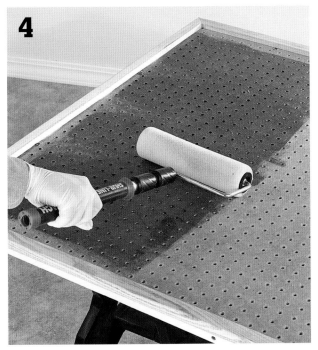

4

Paint or top coat the pegboard. You can leave the pegboard unfinished, if you prefer, but a coat of paint or varnish protects the composite material from nicks and dings and hardens it around the hole openings so the holes are less likely to become elongated. A paint roller and short-nap sleeve make quick work of the job.

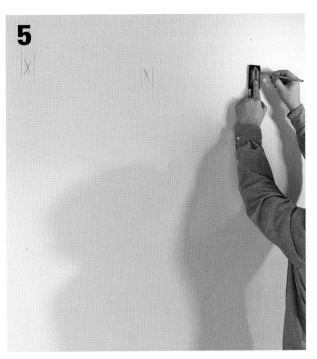

5

Locate and mark wall studs if your garage wall has a wall covering. Make sure the marks extend above and below the pegboard location so you can see them once the pegboard is positioned on the wall.

6

Tack the pegboard and frame to the wall in the desired location. Drive one 2½" screw partway through the top frame at the center of the pegboard. Place a long level on the top of the pegboard and adjust it to level using the screw as a pivot point.

7

Drive a drywall screw through the top and bottom frame rails at each wall stud location. Drill countersunk pilot holes first. Double-check for level after driving the first screw. Insert hangers as desired.

Slat Wall

A slatted wall system combines easy installation, durability, and a range of hanging accessories to form an integrated solution for most any workshop need. They can be customized for differing load demands, they're fairly easy to install, and they have a more finished appearance with greater durability than pegboard.

Have you ever marveled at those floor-to-ceiling, slatted wall storage systems used for product display in many retail stores? You might not think of that approach as a viable option for your garage, but slatted wall systems are definitely available to consumers—and they're easy to install. The slatted panels are made of PVC or composite material in four or eight inch pieces and in a variety of colors. Panels are packaged in cartons that cover between 30 to 40 square feet of wall space. The panel color is blended through the material, so slatted wall systems never need painting. Panels are washable and waterproof, making them perfect for a damp garage. Best of all, slatted wall systems can be outfitted with a variety of hooks, brackets, baskets, shelving, and even cabinetry to store just about anything. Aside from the hanging accessories, manufacturers also offer color-matched screw plugs, trim pieces for surrounding outlets, switch plates, and baseboard and moldings for accommodating room corners.

Installing a slatted wall system is a straightforward project. The installation methods do vary quite a bit, depending mostly on whether you select standard or heavy-duty products. Whatever the method, you need to locate and mark the wall studs in the project area and snap a plumb chalk line to establish the height of the bottom row of slatted panels. Depending on the system you choose, you can attach the panels by driving screws through them and into the wall studs or by attaching clips to the wall first and hanging the panels on the clips. Panels can be attached end-to-end with interlocking dowels and then hung as longer pieces. Then each subsequent row clips to the row below it for an unbroken, seamless look. Slatted wall panels can be cut, drilled, and sanded with ordinary tools, so there's no special bits or blades to buy.

Tools & Materials ▸

Work gloves	Clamps
Eye protection	Jigsaw (or handsaw)
Tape measure	Drill
Chalk line	Wood glue
Level	Slatted wall panels
Circular saw	Wall clips and
Straightedge	connective dowels
Stepladder	Screws
Stud finder	Barbed dowels
Wood block	Hangers and brackets

How to Install Slat Walls

1

2

Lay out vertical and horizontal reference lines if you are installing the slat wall system on a finished wall. The bottom reference line should be 16" above the floor in most installations. Also mark all wall stud locations. For bare stud wall applications, establish horizontal reference lines, that are parallel to the floor.

Attach installation accessories to the wall if you'll be using them. Here, special hangers are attached at stud locations so the wall slat panels in this heavy-duty system can be positioned accurately. For maximum holding power you will also need to drive screws through the mounting slots in each panel.

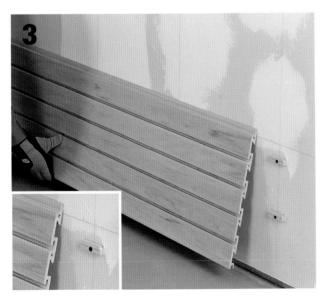

3

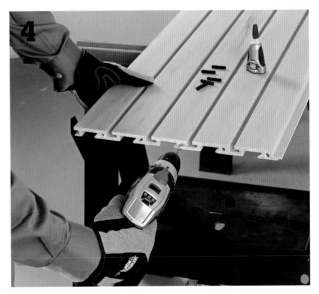

4

Begin installing slat panels, starting at the bottom. Make sure the panel is oriented correctly, with the dovetailed side of the slot facing up so it can slip over the angled edge of the installation accessory (inset photo).

Prepare butted joints between panels. In this system, dowel holes are drilled by enlarging predrilled pilot holes in the panel ends where the panels meet. Barbed dowels are inserted into the dowel holes and glued in place to reinforce the joint. If you do not intend the slat wall to be permanent, do not use glue. The dowel reinforcement is unnecessary if the butt joint between panels falls at a wall stud location.

(continued)

Make butted joints at panel ends by sliding doweled panels together. If the ends do not fit together easily, try rapping the free end of the second panels with a wood block to seat it against the first panel.

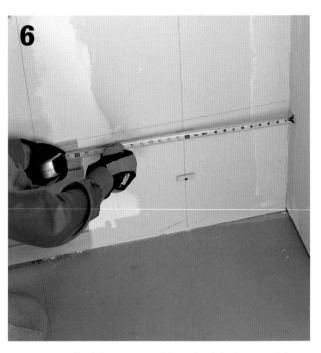

Measure to find the required length of the last panel in the first row of panels (if you are doing a full-wall installation). Subtract ⅛" from the distance to allow for expansion of the PVC plastic or composite panels.

Cut the end panel to length using a circular saw with a straightedge cutting guide. Orient the panel with the good side facing down to minimize tearout from the saw blade. Any general-purpose blade with carbide-tipped teeth will work. *Tip: Set the workpiece on a backer of scrap plywood and set your saw cutting depth so it is slightly deeper than the panel thickness but not deep enough to cut through the backer.*

Install the second course of panels above the first course. Start with a half-length panel to create a staggered running-bond pattern (seams are not aligned among courses).

9

Measure for any cutouts in the panel, such as windows, receptacles, or switches. To find the edges of the cutout, hold the panel directly below the obstruction with the end aligned flush against the panel it will fit against.

10

Make cutouts for obstructions by following the cutting line with a jigsaw or handsaw. If you are making long, straight cuts, you will get a truer cut if you use a circular saw and straightedge guide and then complete the cut at the corners with a jigsaw or handsaw.

11

Install the top row. Most panels are sized so that they will fit onto an 8-ft. wall without cutting to width. But if you need to cut the panels to width, use a circular saw and straightedge cutting guide or a table saw for the job. Make sure to cut from the same side of all cut panels. Install hangers and brackets as desired.

Making Corners ▶

If your slat wall plan calls for making a corner with the material, the easiest way to treat the panels is to butt one panel against another at inside corners or to miter cut the mating panel ends at outside corners. Most slat wall system manufacturers also sell corner trim that may be installed on outside corners for a neater appearance.

APPENDIX A: Shelving

When making shelves for your floor-to-ceiling shelves or utility shelves, choose shelving materials appropriate for the loads they must support. Thin glass shelves or particleboard can easily support light loads, such as decorative glassware, but only the sturdiest shelves can hold a large television set or heavy reference books without bending or breaking.

The strength of a shelf depends on its span—the distance between vertical risers. In general, the span should be no more than 36" long.

Building your own shelves from finish-grade plywood edged with hardwood strips is a good choice for most carpentry projects. Edged plywood shelves are strong, attractive, and much less expensive than solid hardwood shelves.

Tools & Materials ▸

Right-angle drill guide
Drill with bits
Marking gauge
Router
Hammer
Nail set

Shelving material
Scrap pegboard
Pin-style shelf supports
Metal shelf standards
Shelf clips
Finish nails

Attach hardwood edging or moldings to the front face of plywood shelves, using wood glue and finish nails. Position the edging so the top is slightly above the plywood surface, then drill pilot holes and drive finish nails. Use a nail set to countersink the nail heads. Sand the edging so it is smooth with the plywood surface before you finish the shelf. For greater strength, edge plywood shelves with 1 × 2 or 1 × 3 hardwood boards.

¼" glass

Melamine-covered particleboard

¾" pine

¾" finish-grade plywood

¾" hardwood

¾" finish-grade plywood edged with 1 × 2 hardwood

Double-layer plywood edged with hardwood molding

Shelves shown in order of strength

Shelving Examples

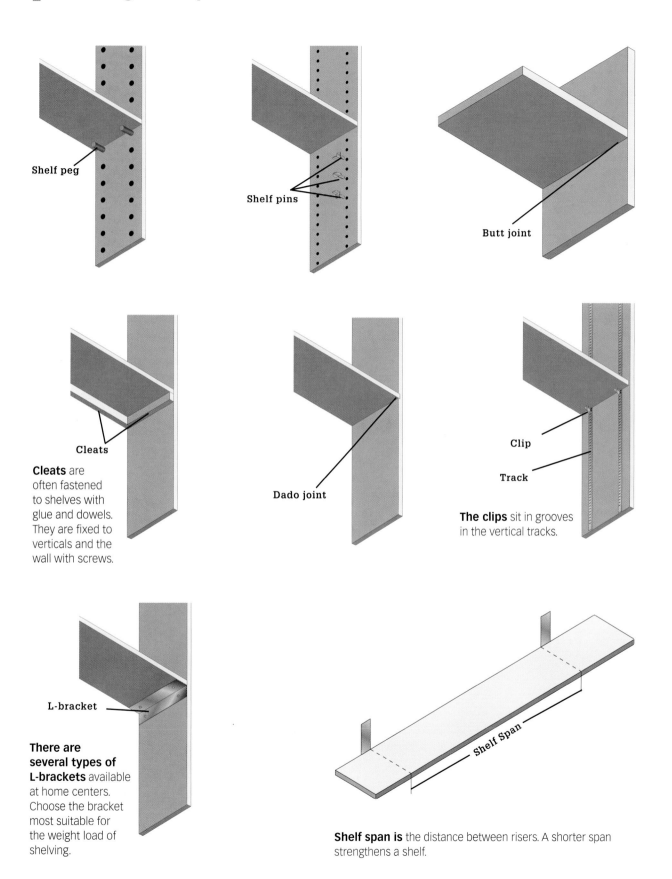

Shelf peg

Shelf pins

Butt joint

Cleats

Cleats are often fastened to shelves with glue and dowels. They are fixed to verticals and the wall with screws.

Dado joint

Clip

Track

The clips sit in grooves in the vertical tracks.

L-bracket

There are several types of L-brackets available at home centers. Choose the bracket most suitable for the weight load of shelving.

Shelf Span

Shelf span is the distance between risers. A shorter span strengthens a shelf.

APPENDIX B: Modular Shelving

Shelving is not a one-size-fits-all proposition. Your beer can collection has entirely different shelving needs from your Encyclopedia Brittanica volumes, which in turn have equally different demands from your paperback novels. The beauty of making your own shelving is that you can easily customize both the size and the support mechanism to your needs.

One good way to customize shelving is to make modular shelves with adjustable supports.

While display shelves can be as narrow as a couple of inches, typical storage shelves range between 11" (bookcases) and 24" (closet or cabinet depth). In this section, you'll learn how to make and finish custom shelves to any width you choose.

Great for closets and utility storage, modular shelves are supported by adjustable pins or brackets so you can easily increase or decrease the space between shelves to meet your storage needs.

Tips for Making Shelves ▶

Rip-cut shelves from sheet stock to the exact width you need. Quality plywood offers the most strength, but for ease of cleaning you'll appreciate melamine-coated particleboard.

Heat-activated veneer edge tape can be applied to the edges of plywood or particleboard shelves for a more finished appearance.

How to Install Pin-style Supports for Adjustable Shelves

1 Mount a drill and ¼" bit in a right-angle drill guide, with the drill-stop set for ⅜" cutting depth. Align a pegboard scrap along the inside face of each shelf standard exactly flush with the end to use as a template. Drill two rows of parallel holes in each riser, about 1½" from the edges of the riser using the pegboard holes as a guide.

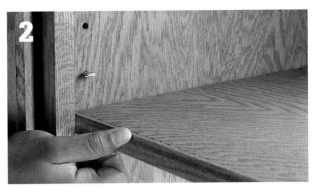

2 When the bookcase or built-in is completed, build shelves that are ¼" shorter than the distance between standards. To mount each shelf, insert a pair of ¼" pin-style shelf supports in each riser.

How to Install Metal Standards for Adjustable Shelves

1 Mark two parallel dado grooves on the inside face of each standard using a marking gauge. Grooves should be at least 1" from the edges.

2 Cut dadoes to depth and thickness of metal tracks using a router. Test-fit tracks, then remove them.

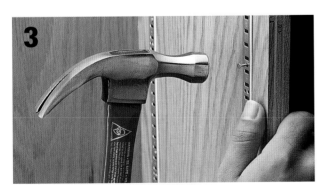

3 After finishing the built-in, cut metal tracks to length to fit into dadoes and attach them using nails or screws provided by the manufacturer. Make sure slots in the tracks are aligned properly so shelves will be level.

4 Make shelves so they are ⅛" shorter than the distance between standards, then insert shelf clips into the slots in the metal tracks, and install the shelves.

APPENDIX C: Wire Shelving

Wire shelving provides a quick and easy solution to a cluttered closet. It lacks adjustability but is nevertheless an inexpensive option to help organize any storage space. Basic wire shelving is attached to walls with support brackets. For entire wall lengths we recommend finding a system that also has return wall brackets (often called side wall brackets) and support clips. Both drywall shelf clips and stud shelf clips are available at home centers. Support brackets placed at stud locations further stabilize the unit.

A slightly advanced style of wire shelving that is increasing in popularity is track mounted. It is available in more styles than standard white vinyl-coated wire shelving. This type of wire shelving consists of a horizontal rail track that supports vertical rails, or the vertical may be directly fastened to the wall. Shelf brackets then snap into the verticals and shelves are set on top of the shelf supports. These systems are viable closet organizers but cannot bear as much weight as wood or melamine systems. The span should be kept to 36" or less and have adequate support—by hitting studs where you can and using toggle bolts every 16".

Tools & Materials ▸

Tape measure	Tape
Level	Drill with bits
Hacksaw	Stud finder
Hammer	Toggle bolts
Shelving system and hardware	1½" drywall screws

How to Install Wire Shelving

MEASURE WALLS AND MARK FOR SHELVING PLACEMENT

Measure the length of the back wall and the side walls. Measure up from the ground to the desired height for the top shelf and draw a level line on each side wall. *Note: The average minimum height above ground is 48".* Mark all stud locations along the back wall and side walls.

CUT WIRE SHELVING

Cut wire shelving to fit between walls using a hacksaw. For shelving lengths greater than 8 feet, cut multiple shelves and connect them with the manufacturer's connectors (which are often sold at home centers that carry wire shelving).

ATTACH SIDE-WALL SUPPORTS

On a side wall, determine placement of the side-wall support according to manufacturer instructions. If instructions are not provided by the manufacturer, fit the support in place on the wire shelf and then, while holding the shelf in place along the level lines, mark the screw hole placements for the side-wall supports on the side walls.

Predrill holes at the marked side-wall support locations. Hold a support in place and insert a toggle bolt through the support into the wall. Repeat with the other side-wall support. *Note: If you can hit a stud, a toggle bolt is not necessary; instead, use a standard 1½" drywall screw.*

Measure your closet and draw a level line 48" up from the floor.

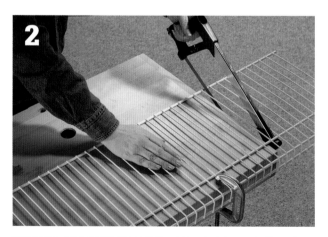

Measure and mark the length of the shelving onto the wire. Cut the wire shelving to length using a hack saw.

3

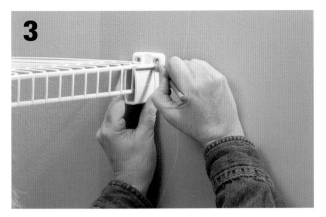

Fit the side-wall bracket in place on the wire shelf and then holding the shelf in place along the level line on the back wall, mark the screw hole placements for the support on the side wall.

4

Mark the clip locations centered on spaces in the wire. (Inset) Mark actual clip-pin hole placement according to manufacturer instructions.

5

Predrill holes for the wall clips to the size and depth recommended by the clip manufacturer.

6

Lower the wire shelving into place. Snap the support clips over the wire shelving.

Place the wire shelving into the side-wall supports. Simply lower the shelving into place until it clicks into the supports. Have a helper hold the shelf so that the two side-wall brackets are not bearing the load of the shelf. Check for level.

MARK THE WALL FOR SUPPORT CLIPS

With wire shelving still fit into the side-wall supports, make a mark approximately every 6" along the wall. Space the marks evenly between studs.

Remove the wire shelving. Hold a clip at each mark, according to manufacturer instructions, and mark the pinhole location. *Note: There is an offset from the level line on the wall that must be taken into account.*

INSERT THE SUPPORT CLIPS IN THE WALL

Predrill holes at the support clip marks on the back wall for the pinhole placement. Insert the wall clips

by pressing the manufacturer pin through the clip and into the wall. Use a hammer to tap stubborn pins into the wall. Lower wire shelving into the side-wall supports until they snap into place. Gently press the back of the shelving into the support clips.

ATTACH SUPPORT BRACKETS

Where possible, align support brackets at stud locations. Mark screw holes on the wall. Determine where the other brackets will go on the wall for a uniform appearance. Space brackets approximately every 16" apart along the back wall.

Attach wall brackets at stud marks, drilling screws through the bracket holes and into the anchors. For brackets that are not fastened to studs, use toggle bolts.

Fasten the other end of the brackets to the wire shelving according to the manufacturer's instructions.

Conversions

Metric Conversions

To Convert:	To:	Multiply by:
Inches	Millimeters	25.4
Inches	Centimeters	2.54
Feet	Meters	0.305
Yards	Meters	0.914
Square inches	Square centimeters	6.45
Square feet	Square meters	0.093
Square yards	Square meters	0.836
Ounces	Milliliters	30.0
Pints (U.S.)	Liters	0.473 (Imp. 0.568)
Quarts (U.S.)	Liters	0.946 (Imp. 1.136)
Gallons (U.S.)	Liters	3.785 (Imp. 4.546)
Ounces	Grams	28.4
Pounds	Kilograms	0.454

To Convert:	To:	Multiply by:
Millimeters	Inches	0.039
Centimeters	Inches	0.394
Meters	Feet	3.28
Meters	Yards	1.09
Square centimeters	Square inches	0.155
Square meters	Square feet	10.8
Square meters	Square yards	1.2
Milliliters	Ounces	.033
Liters	Pints (U.S.)	2.114 (Imp. 1.76)
Liters	Quarts (U.S.)	1.057 (Imp. 0.88)
Liters	Gallons (U.S.)	0.264 (Imp. 0.22)
Grams	Ounces	0.035
Kilograms	Pounds	2.2

Converting Temperatures

Convert degrees Fahrenheit (F) to degrees Celsius (C) by following this simple formula: Subtract 32 from the Fahrenheit temperature reading. Then, multiply that number by $5/9$. For example, $77°F - 32 = 45$. $45 \times 5/9 = 25°C$.

To convert degrees Celsius to degrees Fahrenheit, multiply the Celsius temperature reading by $9/5$. Then, add 32. For example, $25°C \times 9/5 = 45$. $45 + 32 = 77°F$.

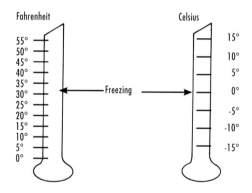

Metric Plywood Panels

Metric plywood panels are commonly available in two sizes: 1,200 mm × 2,400 mm and 1,220 mm × 2,400 mm, which is roughly equivalent to a 4 × 8-ft. sheet. Standard and Select sheathing panels come in standard thicknesses, while Sanded grade panels are available in special thicknesses.

Standard Sheathing Grade		Sanded Grade	
7.5 mm	(5/16 in.)	6 mm	(4/17 in.)
9.5 mm	(3/8 in.)	8 mm	(5/16 in.)
12.5 mm	(1/2 in.)	11 mm	(7/16 in.)
15.5 mm	(5/8 in.)	14 mm	(9/16 in.)
18.5 mm	(3/4 in.)	17 mm	(2/3 in.)
20.5 mm	(13/16 in.)	19 mm	(3/4 in.)
22.5 mm	(7/8 in.)	21 mm	(13/16 in.)
25.5 mm	(1 in.)	24 mm	(15/16 in.)

Lumber Dimensions

Nominal - U.S.	Actual - U.S. (in inches)	Metric
1 × 2	3/4 × 1 1/2	19 × 38 mm
1 × 3	3/4 × 2 1/2	19 × 64 mm
1 × 4	3/4 × 3 1/2	19 × 89 mm
1 × 5	3/4 × 4 1/2	19 × 114 mm
1 × 6	3/4 × 5 1/2	19 × 140 mm
1 × 7	3/4 × 6 1/4	19 × 159 mm
1 × 8	3/4 × 7 1/4	19 × 184 mm
1 × 10	3/4 × 9 1/4	19 × 235 mm
1 × 12	3/4 × 11 1/4	19 × 286 mm
1 1/4 × 4	1 × 3 1/2	25 × 89 mm
1 1/4 × 6	1 × 5 1/2	25 × 140 mm
1 1/4 × 8	1 × 7 1/4	25 × 184 mm
1 1/4 × 10	1 × 9 1/4	25 × 235 mm
1 1/4 × 12	1 × 11 1/4	25 × 286 mm
1 1/2 × 4	1 1/4 × 3 1/2	32 × 89 mm
1 1/2 × 6	1 1/4 × 5 1/2	32 × 140 mm
1 1/2 × 8	1 1/4 × 7 1/4	32 × 184 mm
1 1/2 × 10	1 1/4 × 9 1/4	32 × 235 mm
1 1/2 × 12	1 1/4 × 11 1/4	32 × 286 mm
2 × 4	1 1/2 × 3 1/2	38 × 89 mm
2 × 6	1 1/2 × 5 1/2	38 × 140 mm
2 × 8	1 1/2 × 7 1/4	38 × 184 mm
2 × 10	1 1/2 × 9 1/4	38 × 235 mm
2 × 12	1 1/2 × 11 1/4	38 × 286 mm
3 × 6	2 1/2 × 5 1/2	64 × 140 mm
4 × 4	3 1/2 × 3 1/2	89 × 89 mm
4 × 6	3 1/2 × 5 1/2	89 × 140 mm

Liquid Measurement Equivalents

1 Pint	= 16 Fluid Ounces	= 2 Cups
1 Quart	= 32 Fluid Ounces	= 2 Pints
1 Gallon	= 128 Fluid Ounces	= 4 Quarts

Drill Bit Guide

Twist Bit	Self-piloting	Spade Bit	Adjustable Counterbore	Hole Saw

  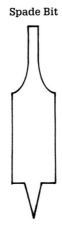 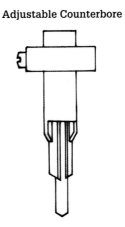 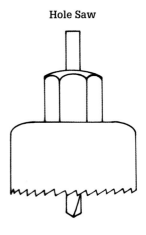

Counterbore, Shank & Pilot Hole Diameters

Screw Size	Counterbore Diameter for Screw Head	Clearance Hole for Screw Shank	Pilot Hole Diameter	
			Hard Wood	Soft Wood
#1	.146 9/64	5/64	3/64	1/32
#2	1/4	3/32	3/64	1/32
#3	1/4	7/64	1/16	3/64
#4	1/4	1/8	1/16	3/64
#5	1/4	9/64	5/64	1/16
#6	5/16	5/32	3/32	5/64
#7	5/16	5/32	3/32	5/64
#8	3/8	11/64	1/8	3/32
#9	3/8	11/64	1/8	3/32
#10	3/8	3/16	1/8	7/64
#11	1/2	3/16	5/32	9/64
#12	1/2	7/32	9/64	1/8

Abrasive Paper Grits - (Aluminum Oxide)

Very Coarse	Coarse	Medium	Fine	Very Fine
12 - 36	40 - 60	80 - 120	150 - 180	220 - 600

Photo Credits

p. 3 (top left) IKEA
p. 6 (all) Aristokraft
p. 7 (top left) Closet Maid, (top right) IKEA, (lower) Eric Roth
p. 8 (all) Aristokraft
p. 9 (top) IKEA, (lower left) Kohler, (lower right) Decolav
p. 10 (top left) IKEA, (top right) Closet Maid
p. 11 (top) California Closets, (lower left) IKEA, (lower right & inset) California Closets
p. 12 (top) Photolibrary, (lower left) IKEA, (lower right) California Closets
p. 13 (top) California Closets, (lower) IKEA
p. 14 (top) California Closets, (lower left) Closet Maid, (lower right) IKEA
p. 15 (top left) Schulte, (top right, lower) California Closets

p. 18 (all) iStock
p. 29 Shutterstock
p. 30 (left) Shutterstock, (right) Diamond Cabinets
p. 32 (far right) Aristokraft
p. 33 (left) Schulte, (top right, middle) Hettich, (lower right) IKEA
p. 61 IKEA
p. 62 Kohler
p. 63 (top left & right, lower left) Kohler
p. 65 (top two) Kohler
p. 87 Merillat
p. 88 Photolibrary
p. 89 (lower two) Room and Board
p. 90 (top) Photolibrary, (lower) California Closets
p. 91 (top left) California Closets, (top right) Schulte, (lower left) Closet Maid, (lower right) Schulte

p. 96 California Closets
p. 123 Shelley Metcalf
p. 124 (left) Shelley Metcalf, (right) Alamy
p. 125 (top left) Beateworks inc./ Alamy, (top right, lower right) IKEA
p. 126 (top) Room and Board, (lower) Closet Maid,
p. 127 (top) Closet Maid, (lower left) iStock, (lower right) Closet Maid
p. 159 Swiss Trax
p. 161 (all) IKEA
p. 162 (top) Photolibrary (inset) Closet Maid, (lower) Closet Maid
p. 163 (top left) iStock, (lower left) IKEA
p. 203 iStock
p. 222 California Closets

Resources

Black & Decker Corp.
Power tools
800-544-6986
www.blackanddecker.com

Rockler Woodworking and Hardware
Pull-down Shelving System, page 58
800-279-4441
www.rockler.com

Contributors

Alamy/www.alamy.com
p. 124 (right), 125 (top left)

Aristokraft Cabinetry
www.aristokraft.com
p. 6 (all), 8 (all), 32 (far right),

California Closets / 888 255 5895 / www.californiaclosets.com
p. 11 (top and lower right), 11 (lower right), 13 (top), 14 (top), 15 (top right, lower), 90 (lower), 96, 222

Closet Maid / 800 874 0008 / www.closetmaid.com
p. 7 (top left), 10 (top right, lower and inset), 14 (lower left), 91 (lower left), 127 (lower left), 162 (top photo inset)

Decolav / 561 274 2110 / www.decolav.com
p. 9 (lower right)

IKEA Home Furnishings / www.ikea.com
p. 7 (top right), 9 (top), 10 (top left), 11 (lower left), 12 (lower left), 13 (lower), 14 (lower right), 33 (lower right), 61, 125 (top right, lower right), 161 (all), 163 (lower left)

IStockphoto / www.istockphoto.com
p. 18 (all), 29, 203

Kohler / 800 456 4537 / www.kohler.com
p. 9 (lower left), 62, 63 (top left & right, lower left), 65 (top two)

Room & Board, Modern furniture and accessories
www.roomandboard.com
p. 89 (lower two), 126 (top)

Schulte / 800 669 3225 / www.schultestorage.com
p. 33 (left), 91 (top right, lower right)

Swisstrax, Inc. / 866 748 7940 / www.swissfloors.com
p. 159

Merillat (cabinets) / www.merillat.com
p. 87

Shelley Metcalf, photographer/ 619 281 0049,
email Shelley.Metcalf@cox.net
p. 123, 124 (left)

Photolibrary, Stock photography / www.photolibrary.com
p. 88, 90 (top), 162 (top)

Eric Roth, photographer / www.ericrothphoto.com
p. 7 (lower)

Index

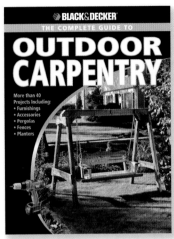
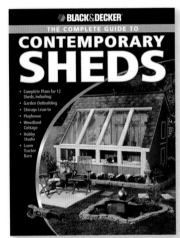
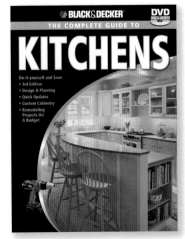